Rust Programming Language for IoT

The Complete Guide to Developing Secure and Efficient Smart Devices

Jeff Stuart

1

Discover Other Books in the Series

"Rust Programming Language for Beginners: The Ultimate Beginner's Guide to Safe and Fast Programming"

"Rust Programming Language for Operating Systems: Build Secure and High-Performance Operating Systems in Rust"

"Rust Programming language for Network: Build Fast, Secure, and Scalable Systems"

"Rust Programming Language for Web Assembly: Build Blazing-Fast, Next-Gen Web Applications"

"Rust Programming Language for Web Development: Building High-Performance Web Applications and APIs"

"Rust Programming Language for Blockchains: Build Secure, Scalable, and High-Performance Distributed Systems"

"Rust Programming Language for Cybersecurity: Writing Secure Code to Implementing Advanced Cryptographic Solutions"

For more information, or to book an event, contact : (Email & Website)

Book design by Jeff Stuart
Cover design by Jeff Stuart

Disclaimer

The information provided in "***Rust Programming for IoT: The Complete Guide to Developing Secure and Efficient Smart Devices***" by Jeff Stuart is intended solely for educational and informational purposes.

Introduction

In an era where the Internet of Things (IoT) is revolutionizing our daily interactions, the demand for secure, efficient, and reliable smart devices has reached unprecedented heights. From smart home innovations that enhance our living environments to industrial IoT solutions that improve operational productivity, developers face the challenge of crafting inventive solutions that unlock the full potential of connectivity.

However, significant advancements bring with them considerable responsibilities. Developers must navigate a complex landscape filled with security vulnerabilities, resource constraints, and diverse hardware configurations.

This is where Rust demonstrates its strengths. As a systems programming language that prioritizes safety and performance, Rust is particularly well-equipped to tackle the challenges inherent in IoT development. Its robust protections against data races and memory-related issues, combined with zero-cost abstractions, make it an ideal choice for building the next generation of smart devices.

Whether you are a seasoned developer looking to expand your expertise or a newcomer eager to embark on this exciting journey, "Rust Programming for IoT: The Complete Guide to Developing Secure and Efficient Smart Devices" is designed to equip you with the essential knowledge and skills necessary to excel in the IoT domain.

In this comprehensive guide, we will explore the fundamental principles of Rust and delve into its powerful features that facilitate the development of secure and efficient applications. Beginning with an introduction to the core concepts of the language, we will gradually address IoT-specific topics, including hardware interfacing, embedded systems management, and data integrity assurance. Through practical examples, hands-on projects, and insightful best practices, you will gain valuable experience in creating smart devices that leverage the full potential of Rust.

Furthermore, security will be a central theme in our exploration. As IoT devices become increasingly embedded in our lives, ensuring their security is of utmost importance. By the end of this guide, you will not only be proficient in Rust programming for IoT applications but also empowered to contribute to a safer and more efficient technological landscape. Let's embark on this journey together, and unlock the vast possibilities that lie at the intersection of Rust and the Internet of Things.

Chapter 1: Introduction to Rust Programming for IoT

The Internet of Things (IoT) is revolutionizing the way we engage with devices and systems. It consists of a network of tangible objects that are outfitted with sensors, software, and various technologies, enabling data exchange via the internet. These objects range from home appliances and wearable technology to industrial machinery, and they have the ability to communicate autonomously, facilitating real-time data analysis and automation.

The rapid expansion of IoT has led to an increased demand for programming languages that are robust, dependable, and efficient. As the complexity of IoT systems grows, the need for languages that prioritize safety, performance, and concurrency becomes more pressing. In this regard, Rust stands out as a significant asset in the IoT landscape.

1.2 Why Choose Rust for IoT Development?

Rust, a systems programming language developed by Mozilla, has proven to be a language that merges speed with safety—two critical characteristics for IoT applications. Below are several compelling reasons to consider Rust for IoT development:

1.2.1 Guaranteed Memory Safety without Garbage Collection

One of Rust's defining features is its strong emphasis on memory safety. By enforcing strict ownership and borrowing rules at compile time, Rust greatly minimizes the risk of common programming mistakes, such as null pointer dereferencing and buffer overflows. This is particularly crucial for IoT devices that may operate in resource-constrained environments, where system failures or unpredictable behavior can have serious consequences.

1.2.2 Exceptional Performance

Rust is engineered for high performance. Its zero-cost abstractions ensure that higher-level constructs do not impose runtime overhead. For IoT devices, where processing power and energy efficiency are critical, this means that Rust applications can operate very close to the hardware while still ensuring safety.### 1.2.3 Concurrency

Concurrency is essential in IoT systems since multiple devices and sensors often need to operate simultaneously. Rust's ownership model allows for safe concurrent programming, enabling developers to write efficient multithreaded applications without the typical race conditions that plague other languages.

1.2.4 Cross-Platform Support

IoT devices come in all shapes and sizes, with various hardware architectures and operating systems. Rust's powerful cross-compilation capabilities enable developers to target diverse platforms, from low-power microcontrollers to powerful single-board computers.

1.2.5 A Growing Ecosystem

Rust's ecosystem is rapidly growing, with a robust set of libraries and tools tailored for IoT development. Crates such as `embedded-hal` facilitate hardware abstraction for embedded systems, while libraries like

`Tokio` enable asynchronous network programming, which is crucial for IoT applications that rely on real-time data streams.

1.3 Getting Started with Rust for IoT

Before diving into Rust for IoT applications, it's essential to set up a proper development environment. The following sections outline the necessary steps to get started.

1.3.1 Installing Rust

Rust can be easily installed using `rustup`, a tool for managing Rust versions and associated tools. Simply run the following command in your terminal:

```bash
curl --proto '=https' --tlsv1.2 -sSf https://sh.rustup.rs | sh
```

This command will download and configure Rust on your machine, providing access to the compiler (`rustc`), package manager (`cargo`), and standard libraries.

1.3.2 Working with Embedded Rust

For IoT applications, developers often work with microcontrollers. To get started, consider using embedded development boards such as Arduino, Raspberry Pi, or ESP32. Rust's embedded ecosystem includes several crates aimed at making development on these platforms more straightforward.

1.3.2.1 Setting Up `embedded-rust`

To set up a new embedded project, you can create a new Cargo project and specify the appropriate dependencies in your `Cargo.toml` file. Below is a simple example for an embedded project using the

`panic-halt` crate, which provides a simple panic handler for embedded programming.

```toml [dependencies] embedded-hal = "0.2"

panic-halt = "0.2"

```

1.3.3 Exploring Rust's Documentation and Community

Rust has an excellent set of documentation and a vibrant community, making it easy for newcomers to get help and share ideas. Resources like the Rust Book, the Rustlings exercises, and forums such as the Rust Users Forum and Discord servers provide ample opportunities for learning and collaboration.

The combination of Rust's memory safety, performance, and concurrency make it an exceptional choice for developing reliable and efficient IoT solutions. With these tools in hand, you are well on your way to harnessing the power of Rust for IoT development, paving the way for innovation in an increasingly connected world.

The Power of Rust Programming for IoT Development

This chapter explores the unique features and benefits of Rust that make it particularly powerful for IoT applications, addressing its advantages in terms of memory safety, concurrency, performance, and community support.

1. Memory Safety Without a Garbage Collector

One of the most striking features of Rust is its approach to memory management. Rust offers memory safety guarantees through a strict ownership model, ensuring that data races and null pointer dereferences are virtually eliminated without the need for a garbage collector.

1.1 Ownership and Borrowing

In Rust, each piece of data has a unique owner, which reduces the chances of dangling pointers and data corruption. The borrowing feature allows developers to temporarily use data without taking ownership, providing greater control over memory usage. For IoT devices, where hardware resources are often limited, this efficiency is crucial. Preventing memory leaks and ensuring that memory usage is predictable leads to more robust applications, particularly in environments where stability is paramount.

1.2 Zero-Cost Abstractions

Rust's zero-cost abstractions mean that developers can write high-level code without incurring runtime penalties. This is particularly important for IoT development, as many applications require real-time performance. By allowing developers to express complex ideas without sacrificing efficiency, Rust empowers them to create sophisticated systems that run efficiently on constrained devices.

2. Concurrency Made Easy

As the number of interconnected devices increases, the need for efficient concurrency becomes critical in IoT applications. Rust's concurrency model is designed to make it easier to write safe concurrent code, eliminating common pitfalls often found in traditional multi-threaded programming.

2.1 Fearless Concurrency

Rust's concurrency model allows developers to work with threads without fear of race conditions. The compiler enforces strict rules that prevent data from being accessed simultaneously in unsafe ways. This ensures that IoT devices can handle multiple tasks concurrently, such as processing sensor data while maintaining network connectivity, without risking data integrity.

2.2 Asynchronous Programming

With Rust's async/await syntax, developers can build highly responsive applications that leverage asynchronous programming effectively. In IoT, devices frequently interact with networks, sensors, and other devices. Asynchronous programming helps to manage these interactions without blocking the main execution thread, leading to smoother operation and a better user experience.

3. Performance Optimization

Many IoT devices operate with limited computational resources and power constraints. Rust shines in delivering performance that rivals C and C++ while being safer to use.

3.1 Low Overhead

Rust's compilation strategy allows developers to write code that compiles down to highly optimized machine code. This low overhead is critical for devices where every

CPU cycle and byte of memory counts. For instance, edge devices that perform local data processing need to do so quickly to reduce latency and bandwidth consumption when communicating with remote servers.

3.2 Fine-Grained Control over System Resources

Rust provides low-level control over hardware resources, making it an ideal choice for embedded systems. Developers can write code that interfaces directly with hardware components, manage memory layout, and optimize performance without having to compromise safety. This level of control is particularly beneficial in UIot applications that require direct manipulation of sensors, actuators, and other devices.

4. Growing Ecosystem and Community

Rust is not only powerful but also comes with an expanding ecosystem that supports IoT development. The growing number of libraries and frameworks targeted at IoT, combined with active community engagement, makes it easier for developers to find solutions and share knowledge.

4.1 Libraries for IoT

Libraries like `tokio`, `async-std`, and `serde` facilitate networking, asynchronous operations, and data serialization, essential features for modern IoT devices. The availability of specialized libraries and crates for microcontrollers, such as the `no_std` environment, further enhances Rust's suitability for IoT applications.

4.2 Community and Support

Rust has a vibrant and welcoming community, evident in its well-maintained documentation, forums, and online resources. The community is particularly adept at addressing challenges faced by developers in niche areas like IoT, making it easier for newcomers to find help and navigate the complex landscape of IoT development.

By combining memory safety guarantees with efficient resource management, Rust enables developers to build reliable and responsive IoT applications. As the IoT landscape continues to mature and evolve, adopting Rust can provide developers with the tools they need to push the boundaries of innovation while ensuring the safety and stability of their devices.

Setting Up the Rust Environment for IoT

Rust, known for its memory safety, speed, and concurrency capabilities, is emerging as a strong contender in IoT development. In this chapter, we will guide you through setting up a complete Rust environment tailored specifically for IoT applications, covering everything from installation to configuring tools and libraries essential for your embedded projects.

1. Understanding the Requirements

Before diving into the installation process, it is important to understand the requirements for developing IoT applications with Rust. IoT devices often have constraints in terms of memory, processing power, and energy consumption. Thus, the Rust environment must support cross-compilation, provide lightweight libraries, and enable efficient access to hardware.

Key Elements to Consider:

Cross-Compilation: Since many IoT devices run on architectures such as ARM, MIPS, or RISC-V, your development environment should support cross-compiling your applications for these target architectures.

Lightweight Libraries: Utilize libraries that cater to embedded system needs, like `no_std` for minimal runtime.

Hardware Abstraction: Familiarity with peripheral access crates (PACs) and Software Component Libraries (SCLs) to properly interface with the hardware.

2. Installing the Rust Toolchain

The first step to setting up your Rust environment is to install the Rust toolchain. Rust provides an official install tool called `rustup`, which manages Rust versions and associated tools.

Steps to Install Rust:

Install Rustup: Open your terminal and run:

```bash
curl --proto '=https' --tlsv1.2 -sSf https://sh.rustup.rs | sh
```

Follow the on-screen instructions.

Adjust Your Path: If prompted, add the Rust binary path to your system's PATH environment variable. This allows you to run Rust binaries from any terminal session.

Verify Installation: Once the installation is complete, verify it by running:

```bash
```

rustc --version

```

You should see the version of Rust that you just installed.
## 3. Installing the Required Dependencies

Rust for IoT often requires additional dependencies to maximize the capabilities of the toolchain. Below are the necessary components to install and configure.

### Key Additions:

- **Cargo**: Rust's package manager is installed automatically with Rustup. You can confirm its existence

by running:

```bash

cargo --version

```

- **Cross-Compile Targets**: When building for specific architectures, you need to add the corresponding target. For example, to add support for `arm-unknown-linux-gnueabi`, you can run:

```bash

rustup target add arm-unknown-linux-gnueabi

```

- **Additional Tools**: Install `gcc`, `gdb`, and any specific tools that cater to your target device. Depending on your OS:

```bash

# For Debian/Ubuntu

sudo apt-get install gcc-arm-none-eabi gdb-multiarch
```

4. Setting Up an Embedded Project

Creating a new embedded project requires special configuration to accommodate the constraints of IoT devices. Below are the steps to set up a simple IoT project in Rust.

Steps to Create a New Project:

Create a New Cargo Project:

```bash
cargo new iot_project --bin cd iot_project
```

Modify `Cargo.toml`:

Update your `Cargo.toml` to include relevant dependencies. For instance, you might want to use the

`embedded-hal` crate for hardware abstraction:

```toml [dependencies]
embedded-hal = "0.2.6"
```

Ensure to also include any chosen crates that fit your project's needs.

Configuring the `main.rs` File:

Depending on your target device, initialize the device peripherals in `src/main.rs` and use the `no_std` library as necessary:

19
```

```rust
#![no_std] #![no_main]
use embedded_hal::digital::v2::OutputPin;
#[cortex_m_rt::entry]
fn main() -> ! {
// Initialize hardware peripherals and your logic
}
```

5. Debugging and Flashing the Device

Debugging IoT applications is crucial, as many issues cannot be replicated outside the hardware environment. Here's how to set up debugging tools and flash your software onto the device:

Flashing and Debugging Tools:

OpenOCD: If using a JTAG/SWD programmer, OpenOCD facilitates debugging. Check your specific programmer's documentation for setup.

Monitoring Output: Use tools like `probe-rs` for flashing and debugging through a debug probe:

```bash
cargo install probe-rs-cli
```

Flashing Your Application:

```bash
probe-rs-cli load --chip YOUR_CHIP_NAME target/arm-unknown-linux-gnueabi/debug/iot_project
```

Setting up the Rust environment for IoT enhances your ability to create fast, efficient, and safe applications for a wide array of devices. While the initial setup may seem complex, leveraging the robustness of Rust, combined with its community support and ecosystems, will ultimately lead to enhanced productivity and fewer errors in production.

Chapter 2: Fundamentals of Embedded Systems

This chapter dives deep into the fundamentals of embedded systems in Rust, exploring aspects such as the architecture of embedded devices, the Rust programming model, and best practices for harnessing Rust's benefits in IoT applications.

2.1 Understanding Embedded Systems ### 2.1.1 What are Embedded Systems?

Embedded systems are specialized computing systems that perform dedicated functions within larger mechanical or electrical systems. These systems are often constrained in resources, such as processing power, memory, and energy consumption. Examples of embedded systems include microcontrollers in household appliances, automotive control systems, and medical devices.

2.1.2 Architecture of Embedded Systems

Embedded systems vary widely in architecture, but they generally consist of the following primary components:

Microcontroller or Microprocessor: The core of the embedded system, responsible for executing code and managing operations.

Memory: This includes RAM (for temporary data storage) and ROM (for permanent storage of firmware).

Input/Output Interfaces: Mechanisms for communication between the embedded system and the external world, including sensors, actuators, and communication modules.

Power Supply: Essential for operation, often constrained to battery efficiency or specific voltage requirements.

The interaction between these components is crucial for system reliability and efficiency, especially in IoT environments where connectivity and real-time processing are critical.

2.2 The Rise of Rust in Embedded Systems ### 2.2.1 Why Rust?

Rust is a systems programming language that emphasizes safety and concurrency without sacrificing performance. Key features that make Rust a strong candidate for embedded systems in IoT include:

Memory Safety: Rust's ownership model prevents common memory-related issues (like null pointer dereferencing and buffer overflows) at compile time, significantly reducing the risk of runtime crashes—a crucial consideration for safety-critical embedded applications.

Concurrency: Rust's fearless concurrency model aids in developing multi-threaded applications safely, making it suitable for IoT devices that handle multiple tasks simultaneously.

Performance: Rust compiles to native code, ensuring that the performance is comparable to that of C and C++ while enabling safer programming practices.

2.2.2 The Rust Embedded Ecosystem

The Rust Embedded Working Group focuses on developing libraries and tools for embedded development. Some noteworthy projects include:

`embedded-hal`: A Hardware Abstraction Layer that promotes interoperability across various hardware implementations.

`no_std`: Support for programming without a standard library, critical for resource-constrained environments.

`RTIC` (Real-Time Interrupt-driven Concurrency)**: A framework for building concurrent applications for embedded systems, emphasizing real-time capabilities.

2.3 Creating Embedded Systems with Rust ### 2.3.1 Setting Up the Environment

To get started with embedded systems development in Rust, the following steps should be followed:

Install the Rust Toolchain: Using `rustup`, install the stable version of Rust, and set your target architecture. For example, for ARM-based microcontrollers:

```bash
rustup target add thumbv7em-none-eabi
```

Choose a Hardware Platform: Common platforms include STM32, ESP32, and Arduino-compatible boards. Each platform has specific setup requirements.

Development Environment: While you can use any text editor or IDE, tools like Visual Studio Code with Rust extension or Eclipse with the Rust plugin enhance productivity.

2.3.2 Writing Your First Embedded Application

Let's use an LED blinking example to illustrate the basic structure of an embedded application in Rust:

Setup Cargo Project:

```bash
cargo new --bin led_blink cd led_blink
```

Modify `Cargo.toml`:

Add necessary dependencies for embedded development. For example:

```toml
[dependencies] embedded-hal = "0.2"
cortex-m = "0.7"
cortex-m-rt = "0.6"
```

Write Code: In `src/main.rs`, write the blinking logic:

```rust
#![no_std] #![no_main]

use cortex_m_rt::entry;
use embedded_hal::digital::v2::OutputPin;
#[entry]
fn main() -> ! {
// Initialization code for your microcontroller
```

```
let mut led = /* initialization of your LED pin */; loop {

    led.set_high().ok(); // Turn LED on delay(); // Some
    delay function led.set_low().ok(); // Turn LED off delay();
    // Some delay function

}

}
```

Building for Your Target: Cross-compile the application for your specific target architecture via Cargo:

```bash
cargo build --target thumbv7em-none-eabi
```

Flash to the Device: Use appropriate tools (like `openOCD` or `cargo-embed`) to flash the compiled binary onto your embedded device.

2.4 Best Practices for Embedded Systems in Rust ### 2.4.1 Resource Management

Effective resource management is vital in constrained environments. Carefully assess memory usage, especially regarding the stack and heap. Use Rust's ownership and borrowing rules to manage resources efficiently.

2.4.2 Testing and Validation

Testing embedded code is often challenging; however, unit testing in Rust is straightforward. Utilize Rust's powerful testing framework to ensure code reliability and correctness.

2.4.3 Safety and Security Considerations

Given that many IoT devices operate in critical environments, prioritize safety and security. Regularly partition resources and apply Rust's type system to establish clear boundaries that embed safety into the design from the outset.

2.4.4 Documentation and Community Resources

Leverage documentation, such as The Rust Book and resources specific to embedded Rust. Engage with the community through forums and working groups to share knowledge and grow as a developer.

Rust is revolutionizing the embedded systems landscape, particularly for IoT applications. Its emphasis on safety, performance, and concurrency positions it as an attractive alternative to traditional languages.

Basics of Embedded Systems and IoT Architecture

This chapter aims to provide a foundational understanding of embedded systems and IoT architecture, setting the stage for advanced concepts and applications.

1. Understanding Embedded Systems

Embedded systems are specialized computing systems that perform dedicated functions within larger mechanical or electrical systems. Unlike general-purpose computers, embedded systems are designed to execute a specific task or set of tasks with efficiency and reliability. They typically consist of a microcontroller or microprocessor, memory, input/output interfaces, and software that controls the hardware.

1.1 Characteristics of Embedded Systems

Task-Specific: Embedded systems are designed to perform a specific function, such as controlling a washing machine, managing a medical device, or operating automotive safety features.

Real-Time Operation: Many embedded systems operate in real-time, meaning they must process input and produce output within a strict time frame to ensure correct functioning.

Resource Constraints: They usually operate on limited resources, including power consumption, processing power, memory, and size.

Reliability and Stability: Given their critical role, embedded systems need to be highly reliable, ensuring that they function correctly in a variety of conditions.

1.2 Components of Embedded Systems

Microcontroller/Microprocessor: The brain of the embedded system, responsible for executing instructions and processing data. Microcontrollers are often chosen for simpler tasks due to their integrated input/output ports and low power consumption.

Memory: Embedded systems typically use two types of memory: ROM (Read-Only Memory) for firmware that executes the main tasks, and RAM (Random Access Memory) for temporary data storage during operation.

Input/Output Interfaces: These components enable embedded systems to interact with the external environment. This can include sensors (inputs) for data collection and actuators (outputs) for controlling external devices.

Software: This is the set of instructions that dictates how the embedded system operates. It can range from simple control loops to complex algorithms for signal processing.

2. Introduction to the Internet of Things (IoT)

The Internet of Things represents a network of physical devices that are connected to the internet, enabling them to collect, share, and analyze data. The interconnectivity of these devices opens up vast possibilities for automation, efficiency, and innovation across various sectors, including healthcare, agriculture, transportation, and smart cities.

2.1 Key Characteristics of IoT

Connectivity: IoT devices must connect to the internet or other networks to transmit data. This requires a reliable communication infrastructure.

Interactivity: Devices share data with one another and with centralized systems, enhancing responsiveness and functionality.

Autonomy: Many IoT systems are designed for autonomous operation, meaning they can make decisions based on predefined criteria without human input.

Scalability: IoT architectures must efficiently handle a growing number of devices and the data they produce without compromising performance.

2.2 Components of IoT Architecture

The architecture of IoT can be conceptualized into several

layers, each serving a distinct purpose in the ecosystem.

Device Layer: This layer encompasses the physical devices equipped with sensors and actuators. These devices collect data from their environment and perform actions based on that data.

Communication Layer: Responsible for transmitting data between devices and to the cloud or other management systems, this layer can include various protocols, such as Wi-Fi, Bluetooth, Zigbee, and cellular networks.

Edge Computing Layer: This layer processes data closer to the source (i.e., the devices themselves) to reduce latency and bandwidth usage. Edge computing ensures faster response times and can enhance privacy and security.

Data Management Layer: In this layer, data is aggregated, stored, and processed. It often involves cloud computing services that allow large-scale storage and computational power for data analysis.

Application Layer: At the top of the IoT architecture, this layer contains the user-facing applications that utilize the processed data to provide insights, control mechanisms, and interfaces for end-users.

3. The Intersection of Embedded Systems and IoT

Embedded systems are foundational to IoT. While embedded systems can operate independently, their integration into IoT creates a powerful synergy. IoT enhances the functionality of embedded systems by enabling them to communicate and collaborate, thus facilitating smarter applications and services.

3.1 Examples of Embedded Systems in IoT

Many modern devices serve as embedded systems and IoT devices simultaneously. Examples include:

Smart Thermostats: They use sensors to gather temperature data and communicate with cloud services to optimize heating and cooling based on user preferences and external weather data.

Wearable Health Monitors: These devices collect biometric data (such as heart rate and activity levels) and transmit the information to mobile applications for health tracking and analysis.

Smart Agriculture Systems: Equipped with sensors to monitor soil moisture, temperature, and humidity, these systems can automatically adjust irrigation based on environmental conditions, leveraging data analytics for better crop management.

Essential Concepts of Low-Level Programming

Low-level programming efficiently interfaces with hardware, managing memory and system resources directly. Rust, with its unique features, combines the speed and control typical of low-level languages like C and C++ while providing safety features that prevent common programming errors. This chapter will explore essential concepts of low-level programming in Rust, including memory management, unsafe code, concurrency, and interfacing with the operating system.

1. Memory Management

At its core, low-level programming revolves around

memory management. In Rust, memory safety is a primary design goal. The Rust ownership model enforces strict rules on how memory is allocated and deallocated:

1.1 Ownership and Borrowing

Ownership: Each value in Rust is owned by a variable, which is responsible for freeing up memory when the variable goes out of scope.

Borrowing: To allow multiple parts of a program to read or modify resources without transferring ownership, Rust uses a borrowing system. Borrowing can be mutable or immutable. You can borrow a value mutably only once at a time, while immutable borrows can occur simultaneously.

1.2 Lifetimes

Lifetimes are Rust's way of ensuring that references are valid as long as they are being used. By using lifetimes, programmers can indicate how long references to data should be valid, preventing dangling references that can lead to undefined behavior. The compiler uses these lifetime annotations to enforce rules at compile time, reducing the likelihood of runtime errors.

2. Unsafe Code

While the ownership model makes Rust safe, there are scenarios where developers may need the control provided by unsafe operations, especially in systems programming, such as interfacing with hardware or manipulating raw pointers.

2.1 Unsafe Blocks

An `unsafe` block allows you to perform operations that

the Rust compiler cannot guarantee are safe:

```rust
unsafe {
let x: *const i32 = &10; let y: *const i32 = &20;


// Dereferencing a raw pointer (unsafe) println!("Value: {}", *x);
}
```

Using `unsafe` provides a pathway to write low-level code without the borrow checker, but it is essential to ensure that these operations do not lead to memory corruption or undefined behavior.

2.2 Raw Pointers

Rust provides raw pointers (`*const T` and `*mut T`) for scenarios where you might need to bypass Rust's ownership rules. While they offer flexibility, using them requires careful management to avoid issues related to dangling pointers, double frees, and memory leaks.

3. Concurrency

Rust's approach to concurrency is another essential aspect of low-level programming, emphasizing safety without needing a garbage collector.

3.1 The Ownership Model in Concurrency

Rust's ownership model extends to concurrency, allowing multiple threads to access shared data safely. The compiler ensures that data races cannot occur by enforcing strict borrowing rules, guaranteeing that either:

One thread has mutable access to a resource, or

Multiple threads have immutable access to a resource.
3.2 Channels and Mutexes

Rust provides tools such as channels and mutexes for safe inter-thread communication:

Channels: Allow threads to communicate by sending messages. They facilitate ownership transfer and prevent data races.

```rust
use std::sync::mpsc; use std::thread;

let (tx, rx) = mpsc::channel(); thread::spawn(move || {

tx.send("Hello from thread").unwrap();

});
println!("{}", rx.recv().unwrap());
```

Mutex: Provides mutual exclusion, enabling safe access to shared data across threads.

```rust
use std::sync::{Arc, Mutex}; use std::thread;

let counter = Arc::new(Mutex::new(0)); let mut handles = vec![];

for _ in 0..10 {

let counter = Arc::clone(&counter); let handle = thread::spawn(move || {
```

```
let mut num = counter.lock().unwrap();
*num += 1;
});
handles.push(handle);
}
for handle in handles { handle.join().unwrap();
}
println!("Result: {}", *counter.lock().unwrap());
```

4. Interfacing with the Operating System

Rust provides capabilities to interface directly with the operating system, a key requirement for low-level programming. The standard library offers tools to work with processes, threads, and file systems.

4.1 System Calls

Rust allows calling system APIs, enabling low-level operations like interacting with files and processes. The

`std::os` module offers OS-specific functionalities. ### 4.2 Foreign Function Interface (FFI)

Rust easily interfaces with other programming languages, particularly C. With FFI, developers can call C functions and use C libraries, bridging the gap between Rust's safety and existing C codebases.

Example of FFI

Here's a simple example of calling a C function from Rust:

```rust
```

```
// Assuming you have a C library with the following
function:
// int add(int a, int b) { return a + b; }
// To interface with this function from Rust:
extern "C" {
fn add(a: i32, b: i32) -> i32;
}
fn main() { unsafe {
let result = add(5, 7); println!("Result: {}", result);
}
}
```
```

Understanding the essential concepts of low-level programming in Rust is crucial for developers who want to leverage the language's unique combination of performance and safety. Through careful attention to memory management, the controlled use of unsafe code, concurrency mechanisms, and the ability to interact with the operating system, Rust empowers programmers to write efficient, robust low-level applications.
```

Chapter 3: Rust Basics for IoT Developers

With this increase in complexity and the diverse requirements for IoT devices, the choice of programming language becomes critical. Among the many languages available, Rust has emerged as a strong contender. This chapter will introduce you to the fundamental concepts of Rust, its features, and how these can be leveraged in IoT development.

3.1 Introduction to Rust

Rust is a systems programming language that prioritizes safety, performance, and concurrency. It is designed to give developers control over system resources while preventing common pitfalls experienced in many other languages, such as memory leaks and data races. Rust's unique ownership model is its cornerstone, ensuring that memory safety is guaranteed without requiring a garbage collector. This makes Rust particularly well-suited for resource-constrained environments, such as IoT devices.

3.1.1 Why Use Rust for IoT?

Memory Safety: With IoT devices often operating on limited hardware, memory safety is paramount. Rust's borrow checker helps to enforce strict rules around memory usage, mitigating common bugs related to null or dangling pointers.

Performance: Rust offers predictable performance comparable to C and C++ due to its zero-cost abstractions. This means you can write high-level code without sacrificing the low-level control needed for optimal resource utilization.

Concurrency: IoT applications often require handling multiple tasks simultaneously, such as sensor readings, data processing, and network communication. Rust's concurrency model, based on ownership, enables developers to create safe concurrent applications without the fear of data races.

Cross-Platform Development: Rust supports cross-compilation, allowing developers to write code that can run on various hardware architectures commonly found in IoT devices.

Modern Language Features: Rust is equipped with modern programming features such as pattern matching, traits, and an expressive type system, which can enhance the productivity of IoT developers.

3.2 Getting Started with Rust ### 3.2.1 Installation

To get started with Rust, you need to install `rustup`, Rust's installer and version management tool. This can be done by running the following command in your terminal:

```bash
curl --proto '=https' --tlsv1.2 -sSf https://sh.rustup.rs | sh
```

Once installed, you will have access to the Rust compiler (`rustc`), the package manager (`cargo`), and other tools.

3.2.2 Your First Rust Program

Let's write a simple "Hello, World!" program in Rust. Create a new directory and navigate into it:

```bash
mkdir rust_iot_project cd rust_iot_project
```

```
```

Then, create a new Rust file named `main.rs`:

```rust
fn main() {
println!("Hello, World!");
}
```

You can compile and run this program with the following commands:

```bash
rustc main.rs
./main
```

3.2.3 Understanding Rust Syntax

Rust syntax is clean and modern, making it relatively easy for developers coming from other languages such as Python or JavaScript. Here are some basic ingredients of Rust syntax:

- **Variables and Mutability**: Variables are immutable by default. To make a variable mutable, you need to use the `mut` keyword:

```rust
let mut x = 5;
x += 1; // Valid since x is mutable
```

- **Data Types**: Rust has a strong type system. Basic data types include integers, floating-point numbers, booleans, and characters. Complex types like arrays and tuples are also supported:

```rust
let a: i32 = 10; let b: f64 = 20.5; let c: bool = true;

let tuple: (i32, f64) = (5, 10.2);
```

- **Control Flow**: Rust supports standard control flow constructs like `if`, `else`, `for` loops, and `while` loops:

```rust
for i in 0..5 { println!("Iteration: {}", i);

}
```

3.3 Error Handling in Rust

Error handling is a critical aspect of developing IoT applications, especially when dealing with unreliable network connections or sensor data. Rust uses two main types for error handling: `Result` and `Option`.

- **Result**: Represents either success (`Ok`) or failure (`Err`).

```rust
fn divide(numerator: f64, denominator: f64) -> Result<f64, String> { if denominator == 0.0 {

Err("Cannot divide by zero".to_string())

} else {
```

Ok(numerator / denominator)

}

}

```

- **Option**: Represents a value that can be either `Some` or `None`, which is useful for cases where a value might be absent.

```rust
fn find_value(key: &str) -> Option<i32> {

let map = std::collections::HashMap::new();
map.get(key).cloned()

}
```

3.4 Basic I/O and External Libraries

In IoT application development, you often need to interface with hardware and process data from different sources. Rust's standard library provides basic I/O operations, and for more advanced tasks, you can leverage the rich ecosystem of external libraries available through `Cargo`, Rust's package manager.

To include an external library, add it to your project's `Cargo.toml` file:

```toml [dependencies]

serde = "1.0" # For JSON serialization/deserialization
```

To perform tasks such as reading sensors or
```

communicating over a network, libraries such as `tokio` for asynchronous programming, and `serde` for JSON handling are invaluable.

Understanding the basics of Rust is an essential step for IoT developers looking to build robust, efficient, and safe applications. The combination of memory safety, performance, and concurrency features makes Rust an excellent choice for developing applications that run on resource-constrained devices in the ever-evolving landscape of IoT.

Rust Language Fundamentals for IoT Development

With millions of devices connected to the internet, the need for a robust programming language has never been more crucial. Rust, a systems programming language, has risen to prominence due to its emphasis on safety, concurrency, and performance. This chapter delves into the fundamental concepts of Rust that are particularly relevant for IoT development, exploring its features, advantages, and best practices for building IoT applications.

1. Understanding Rust: A Brief Overview

Rust was developed by Mozilla with a focus on safety and concurrency. It is designed to provide memory safety without using garbage collection, which is particularly advantageous for resource-constrained devices in IoT. Let's explore some core attributes of Rust that make it suitable for IoT development:

1.1 Memory Safety

Rust's ownership model ensures that data is owned by a

single variable at a time, preventing data races and null pointer dereferencing. The strict compile-time checks prevent common bugs, such as buffer overflows and use-after-free errors, which can lead to vulnerabilities in IoT devices.

1.2 Performance

Rust compiles to native code, enabling high-performance applications that are critical for IoT devices. Its zero-cost abstractions mean that developers can write high-level code without sacrificing performance, making it an excellent choice for both high-end gateways and low-power embedded systems.

1.3 Concurrency

Rust's approach to concurrent programming allows developers to write safe multithreaded code. This is essential for IoT applications that often require simultaneous processing of multiple sensor inputs and network communications.

2. Getting Started with Rust

Before delving into IoT-specific applications, let's look at the essentials of the Rust programming language. ### 2.1 Installation

Rust can be easily installed using 'rustup', a toolchain installer. Start by visiting the official Rust website and following the installation instructions:

```bash
curl --proto '=https' --tlsv1.2 -sSf https://sh.rustup.rs | sh
```

After installation, ensure the Rust environment is correctly set up by running:

```bash
rustc --version
```

2.2 Basic Syntax

Understanding the syntax is crucial for any programming language. Here are some of the fundamental constructs in Rust:

- **Variables and Mutability**: Variables in Rust are immutable by default. To declare a mutable variable, use the `mut` keyword.

```rust
let mut temperature = 25;

temperature += 1; // temperature is now 26
```

- **Data Types**: Rust has various data types, including integers, floating-point numbers, booleans, and strings. Arrays and tuples provide compound data types.

```rust
let numbers: [i32; 5] = [1, 2, 3, 4, 5];

let tuple: (i32, f64) = (42, 6.7);
```

- **Control Flow**: Rust supports standard control flow constructs such as loops and conditional statements.

```rust
for number in &numbers { println!("{}", number);
}
```

2.3 Functions and Error Handling

Functions are defined using the `fn` keyword, and Rust emphasizes explicit error handling through the

`Result` and `Option` types.

```rust
fn divide(a: f64, b: f64) -> Result<f64, String> { if b == 0.0 {
Err("Cannot divide by zero".into())
} else {
Ok(a / b)
}
}
```

3. Rust for IoT Development ### 3.1 Leveraging Crates

The Rust ecosystem includes a rich variety of libraries known as "crates." For IoT development, some relevant crates include:

`tokio`: An asynchronous runtime for writing reliable and fast applications.

`serde`: A framework for serializing and deserializing Rust data structures, useful for handling JSON, BSON, and other data formats.

`embedded-hal`: A hardware abstraction layer that aids in writing portable code for embedded systems.

3.2 Building an IoT Application

Let's illustrate how to build a simple IoT application that reads data from a temperature sensor and sends it over MQTT.

Step 1: Setting Up a New Project Create a new Rust project:

```bash
cargo new iot_sensor cd iot_sensor
```

Add dependencies to your `Cargo.toml`:

```toml
[dependencies]
paho-mqtt = "0.8" # MQTT client

serde = { version = "1.0", features = ["derive"] } # Serialization
```

Step 2: Reading Sensor Data

Assume you have a function that reads from a temperature sensor:

```rust
fn read_temperature() -> f64 {
// Simulate reading from a sensor
22.5 // returning a dummy value
```

```
}
```

Step 3: Sending Data via MQTT

Using the MQTT crate, connect to a broker and publish the sensor data:

```rust
use paho_mqtt as mqtt;

fn main() {

let mqtt_client = mqtt::Client::new("tcp://broker.hivemq.com:1883").unwrap(); mqtt_client.connect(None).unwrap();

loop {

let temperature = read_temperature();

let msg = format!("Temperature: {:.2}", temperature); mqtt_client.publish("home/temperature", msg, mqtt::QOS_1, false).unwrap();


std::thread::sleep(std::time::Duration::from_secs(5));

}
}
```

3.3 Cross-Compilation for Embedded Systems

A crucial aspect of IoT development involves cross-compilation as many IoT devices run on microcontrollers. Rust supports cross-compilation, allowing developers to target different architectures.

Install the required target:

```bash
rustup target add thumbv7em-none-eabihf
```

Use `cargo` to compile your project for the target:

```bash
cargo build --target thumbv7em-none-eabihf
```

By leveraging its features and the capabilities of its ecosystem, developers can build reliable IoT systems capable of handling the demands of connected hardware.

Key Features of Rust for Embedded Systems

This chapter will explore the key features of Rust that make it particularly well-suited for embedded systems development.

Memory Safety Without Garbage Collection

One of the standout features of Rust is its rigorous approach to memory safety, achieved through its ownership model. Unlike languages such as C and C++, which are prone to common pitfalls like buffer overflows and dangling pointers, Rust enforces memory safety at compile time without the need for a garbage collector.

In embedded systems, where resources are often constrained, the absence of a garbage collector is particularly advantageous. Rust's ownership system ensures that memory is automatically reclaimed when it goes out of scope, thus eliminating memory leaks while providing predictability in memory usage — a critical characteristic for real-time systems.

Zero-Cost Abstractions

Rust provides zero-cost abstractions, meaning developers can use high-level features without incurring runtime overhead. This is crucial in embedded systems, where performance is often a key requirement. The ability to write code that is both expressive and efficient allows developers to focus on clear, maintainable code while still interacting directly with the hardware when needed.

Feature-rich abstractions, such as iterators and closures, enable developers to write compact and elegant code. Behind the scenes, Rust's compiler optimizations ensure that these abstractions do not introduce unnecessary overhead, making Rust a powerful contender in resource-limited environments.

Concurrency Without Data Races

Concurrency in embedded systems is often necessary due to the real-time processing of events. Rust's approach to concurrency is integral to its design. The language provides compile-time checks that guarantee data races are avoided, which is a common source of bugs in concurrent programming.

Through ownership and borrowing, Rust ensures that mutable state is accessed by only one thread at a time, while immutable state can be shared freely. This design provides a robust foundation for building concurrent applications without falling into the traps commonly associated with multithreading, thereby enhancing the reliability of embedded systems.

Strong Type System

Rust's strong static type system plays a significant role in reducing runtime errors. By enforcing strict type checking during compilation, many categories of bugs can be detected early in the development process. This feature is essential for embedded systems, where even minor software errors can lead to catastrophic failures in physical devices.

Moreover, Rust's type system supports the creation of expressive APIs that encapsulate complex behavior, allowing developers to work at a higher level of abstraction. This could lead to safer and more maintainable interfaces when dealing with hardware peripherals.

Interoperability With C

Many existing embedded systems are written in C, and Rust is designed to interoperate seamlessly with it. The `extern` keyword in Rust allows developers to call C functions and utilize C libraries, enabling incremental adoption of Rust in legacy systems. This interoperability is essential for integrating Rust into existing projects and reusing established codebases while progressively transitioning to a safer language model.

No Hidden Control Flow

Rust emphasizes clarity in control flow and does not employ hidden control structures such as exceptions. All control paths must handle errors explicitly, which enhances code robustness and predictability. In embedded systems, where system failure can have dire consequences, this approach fosters a clear understanding of error handling practices, leading to more reliable applications.

Compile-Time Performance and Size Optimization

In embedded systems, compile-time performance and binary size are often critical metrics. Rust's powerful optimization capabilities allow developers to tune their applications for maximum efficiency. By leveraging the LLVM backend, Rust can produce optimized binaries that minimize memory usage and maximize execution speed.

Additionally, since Rust allows for fine-grained control over resource allocation, developers can create minimal embedded applications that run within stringent constraints. This capability makes Rust a compelling choice for a broad range of embedded workloads, from microcontrollers to more powerful SoCs (System on Chips).

Community and Ecosystem Support

Since its inception, Rust has cultivated a vibrant and active community. The ecosystem around Rust's embedded programming is growing rapidly, with libraries, tools, and frameworks specifically targeted at embedded systems. The `no_std` environment, which allows Rust to operate without the standard library, enables development for bare-metal systems and microcontrollers.

Projects such as `embedded-hal` (Hardware Abstraction Layer) further illustrate the community's commitment to providing a comprehensive toolkit for embedded developers. With increasing support for microcontroller-specific crates and an active community, developers can leverage existing resources to accelerate their development processes.

In conclusion, Rust brings a plethora of features that align well with the challenges and requirements of embedded systems programming. Its focus on memory safety, concurrency without data races, strong typing, and interoperability with C equips developers with the tools they need to build safe, efficient, and reliable systems.

Chapter 4: Working with Hardware Using Embedded-HAL

The Embedded Hardware Abstraction Layer (Embedded-HAL) framework provides a standard interface for accessing and controlling hardware peripherals across different platforms. This chapter delves into the principles of Embedded-HAL, its architecture, and practical examples that illustrate its application in real- world embedded systems.

4.1 Understanding Embedded-HAL

Embedded-HAL is designed to abstract hardware interactions, allowing developers to write code that is portable across various microcontrollers and platforms. This abstraction not only simplifies the process of interfacing with hardware but also promotes code reusability and maintainability.

4.1.1 Key Concepts

Ports and Traits: The central idea of Embedded-HAL revolves around defining traits for various hardware components — for example, digital pins, timers, I2C, SPI, and UART. Each trait encapsulates operations that can be performed through that specific hardware interface.

Implementations: Each microcontroller may implement these traits differently based on its hardware characteristics. By using traits, developers can write hardware-agnostic code that compiles for any compatible platform with a suitable implementation.

4.1.2 Benefits of Using Embedded-HAL

Portability: Code written with Embedded-HAL can be

easily ported across different microcontrollers and boards.

Modularity: Each hardware operation is encapsulated in traits, making it easier to swap hardware implementations without extensive refactoring of the codebase.

Community Support: Embedded-HAL has a growing ecosystem of libraries and community- contributed implementations, enabling faster development and problem-solving.

4.2 Setting Up the Development Environment

Before diving into practical examples, ensure that you have the following tools set up in your development environment:

Rust Toolchain: Embedded-HAL is primarily used within the Rust programming language, so install the Rust compiler and Cargo package manager if you haven't already.

Embedded Target: You need to set up the toolchain for your target microcontroller (e.g., using `rustup target add thumbv7em-none-eabihf` for ARM Cortex-M).

Cargo-Embedded: It's beneficial to use `cargo-embed`, `cargo-generate`, or other tools that simplify flash and debugging processes in embedded environments.

4.3 Working with Digital Pins

This section demonstrates how to interact with digital I/O pins using Embedded-HAL. ### 4.3.1 Pin Configuration First, consider a scenario where we need to blink an LED connected to a GPIO pin. Here's an example:

```rust
use embedded_hal::digital::v2::{OutputPin, PinState};

struct MyBoard {
led: Pin, // Assume Pin is a type from your specific HAL implementation.
}

impl MyBoard {
fn new() -> Self {

let led = Pin::new(/* configurations */);
led.set_high().unwrap(); // Turn off the LED initially. Self { led }

}
fn blink(&mut self) {

self.led.toggle().unwrap(); // Toggle the state of the LED.

}
}
```

4.3.2 Polling and Timing

To create a blinking effect, you'll also need to implement a simple delay mechanism:

```rust
fn delay_ms(ms: u32) {

let start_time = get_current_time(); // Implement port-specific timing while get_current_time() - start_time < ms {}
```

```
}
```

You can incorporate the delay into your main application loop:

```rust
fn main() {
    let mut board = MyBoard::new();

    loop {
        board.blink(); // Toggle the LED state delay_ms(500); //
        Delay for 500 milliseconds
    }
}
```

4.4 Working with I2C Peripheral

For devices like sensors, communication via I2C is crucial. Let's create an I2C interface. ### 4.4.1 Setting Up I2C

Start by defining the traits for I2C communication:

```rust
use embedded_hal::i2c::blocking::{I2c as BlockingI2C, Write, Read};

struct MySensor<I2C> { i2c: I2C,

    address: u8,
}
```

```rust
impl<I2C> MySensor<I2C> where
I2C: BlockingI2C,
{
fn new(i2c: I2C, address: u8) -> Self { Self { i2c, address }
}
fn read_data(&mut self) -> Result<[u8; 3], I2C::Error> {
let mut buffer = [0; 3];

self.i2c.read(self.address, &mut buffer)?; Ok(buffer)

}
}
```

4.4.2 Using the I2C Sensor

You can now use the `MySensor` struct in your main loop:

```rust
fn main() {

let mut i2c_peripheral = /* instantiate your I2C peripheral */;

let mut sensor = MySensor::new(i2c_peripheral, 0x28);
// Example sensor address

loop {

match sensor.read_data() { Ok(data) => {

// Process your data

}
```

```
Err(err) => {
// Handle error
}
}
delay_ms(1000); // Delay for demonstration
}
}
```
```

In this chapter, we explored how to work with hardware using Embedded-HAL. We discussed the key principles of the framework, highlighted the process of setting up your development environment, and walked through practical examples involving digital pins and I2C communication.

## Introduction to the Embedded-HAL Library

These systems often require real-time performance, energy efficiency, and robustness, making them ideal candidates for programming languages that enable low-level hardware control. Rust has emerged as a strong contender in this space, providing safety and performance without sacrificing direct hardware access.

## 1.2 What is the Embedded-HAL?

The Embedded Hardware Abstraction Layer (Embedded-HAL) represents a key building block in the Rust ecosystem for embedded systems. It aims to provide a common interface for interacting with various hardware components, such as timers, GPIOs (General Purpose
```

Input/Output), I2C, SPI (Serial Peripheral Interface), and more. The concept behind HAL is to abstract the hardware specifics while ensuring that performance and safety—core tenets of Rust—are maintained.

The Embedded-HAL library consists of traits, which define the functionality expected from a specific hardware component. By adhering to these traits, developers can swap out hardware implementations without modifying higher-level code. This means a project can evolve easily—developers can switch microcontrollers or peripherals with less friction.

1.3 Importance of Abstraction in Embedded Systems
Abstraction in embedded systems design plays several critical roles:

Code Reusability: With an abstraction layer, developers can write modular code that can be reused across different projects. By leveraging the traits provided by Embedded-HAL, developers can use the same codebase for multiple devices.

Portability: Applications written with Embedded-HAL can more easily migrate to different hardware platforms. If a project designed around one microcontroller needs to move to another, developers often require minimal changes.

Ease of Testing: By abstracting hardware interactions, it becomes easier to unit test software logic without relying on the actual hardware, promoting better development practices and reducing debugging time.

Collaboration: Teams working on different components can do so asynchronously, as long as they conform to the HAL interface, allowing for smoother project management and integration.

1.4 Key Features of Embedded-HAL

Embedded-HAL boasts several features that make it an attractive choice for embedded Rust programming:

Safety Guarantees: Rust's type system and ownership model ensure that many common bugs (such as null pointer dereferences and data races) are eliminated at compile time.

No Standard Library: Embedded-HAL is designed to work without the standard library, which is crucial for environments with strict resource restrictions.

Feature-rich Traits: It encompasses a multitude of traits that cater to different functionalities—GPIO for digital I/O, Timer for delays and timing operations, UART for serial communication, I2C and SPI for interfacing with peripheral devices, and many others.

Minimal Platform Overhead: The library is lightweight, ensuring that integrating Embedded-HAL into your project doesn't incur significant resource overhead.

1.5 Setting Up Embedded-HAL

Before diving into projects that leverage the Embedded-HAL library, developers should properly set up their development environment:

Install Rust: Ensure that Rust is installed on your machine. This can be achieved via `rustup`, the Rust toolchain installer.

Add Necessary Crates: To use Embedded-HAL, include it in your `Cargo.toml`:

```toml
[dependencies]
embedded-hal = "0.2"  # Check for the latest version in the crates.io
```

Choose a Target: Embedded systems typically target specific platforms. Use the appropriate target specification for your microcontroller or development board.

Choose and Implement a Specific HAL: Various implementations of Embedded-HAL exist, often tailored for specific platforms. For instance, you could use `stm32f1xx-hal` if working with STM32F1 microcontrollers.

The Embedded-HAL library is instrumental for developers and engineers working within the Rust ecosystem who are looking to build efficient, safe, and portable embedded applications. By abstracting hardware interaction through well-defined traits, it allows code to be more maintainable and adaptable to different platforms, thus enhancing the overall development experience.

Writing Your First Hardware Control Program

We're going to explore the unique characteristics of Rust, its safety features, and how they apply to hardware programming. By the end, you will have a foundational understanding that will empower you to build more complex applications.

Why Rust for Hardware Control?

Rust has garnered a reputation for being a "safe systems programming language." This means it offers low-level memory access akin to C and C++, but with a stronger emphasis on safety and concurrency. Key features that make Rust an excellent choice for hardware programming include:

Memory Safety: Rust's ownership model prevents data races and null pointer dereferences, which are common issues in C/C++.

Rich Type System: Rust's strong and expressive type system helps catch errors at compile-time, reducing runtime bugs.

Concurrency: Rust makes it easier to write concurrent and parallel code, allowing better performance on multicore processors.

Setting Up Your Rust Environment

Before we start writing our hardware control program, you'll need to set up your environment. Follow these steps:

Install Rust: Download and install Rust using `rustup`, the Rust installer and version management tool. You can follow the instructions from the official [Rust website](https://www.rust-lang.org/tools/install).

Choose a Target Platform:

Select a microcontroller or embedded system platform, such as Arduino, Raspberry Pi, or STM32.

Ensure you have the requisite toolchain for cross-compilation if you're working on a more complex platform.

Install Additional Tools: For some platforms, you

might need additional tools or libraries such as:

`cargo`: The Rust package manager, which handles project dependencies and builds.

`embedded-hal`: A hardware abstraction layer for embedded systems in Rust.

Set Up Your Project:

To create a new Rust project, run:

```bash
cargo new hardware_control cd hardware_control
```

Writing Your First Hardware Control Program

In this section, we will write a simple program to blink an LED connected to a microcontroller. #### Step 1: Project Structure

When you create a new Cargo project, it generates a basic structure:

```
hardware_control/ Cargo.toml
src/
main.rs
```

The `Cargo.toml` file contains the configuration for your project, while the `main.rs` file is where you will write your code.

Step 2: Modify `Cargo.toml`

Open `Cargo.toml` and add dependencies for the hardware abstraction layer and any other necessary libraries.

```toml
[dependencies] embedded-hal = "0.2"
```

Step 3: Writing the LED Blink Code

Open `src/main.rs` and write your program. The code below assumes you are working with an embedded HAL set up for a specific microcontroller. Replace the placeholder types and methods with those specific to your hardware platform.

```rust
#![no_std] #![no_main]

use panic_halt as _; // Halt on panic

use embedded_hal::digital::v2::OutputPin;

use embedded_hal::timer::CountDown; // For timing, if applicable

#[no_mangle] fn main() -> ! {

// Initialize peripherals (exact code will depend on your platform) let peripherals = ...; // Get your microcontroller's peripherals

// Set up the GPIO pin for the LED

let mut led = peripherals.pins.led.into_output().unwrap();


// Set up a timer

let mut timer = peripherals.timer.constrain(); // Initialize your timer
```

```
loop {
    led.set_high().unwrap();    // Turn LED on
    timer.delay(1.seconds()).unwrap(); // Wait for 1 second

    led.set_low().unwrap();     // Turn LED off
    timer.delay(1.seconds()).unwrap(); // Wait for 1 second
}
}
```

Step 4: Compiling and Uploading

Now it's time to compile and upload your code to the microcontroller. Use the following command:

```bash
cargo build --target=your-target-architecture
```

Replace `your-target-architecture` with your specific target (such as `thumbv7em-none-eabi` for ARM Cortex-M).

To upload the program, you might need specific commands based on your hardware platform (e.g., using

`cargo-embed`, `OpenOCD`, or Arduino IDE). ### Step 5: Running Your Program

Once uploaded, reset your microcontroller. If everything is set up correctly, you should see the LED blinking on and off every second. Congratulations! You've just written your first hardware control program using Rust.

In this chapter, we explored why Rust is an excellent

choice for hardware control programming, set up our development environment, and walked through the process of writing a simple LED blinking program. As you become more familiar with Rust and embedded systems, there will be much more to learn about sensors, actuators, communication protocols, and more complex applications.

Chapter 5: Memory Management and Safety in Rust

In this chapter, we will explore Rust's memory management model, its ownership system, and safety guarantees that distinguish it from other programming languages.

5.1 The Problem of Memory Management

Historically, memory management has presented a myriad of challenges for programmers. Languages like C and C++ give developers direct control over memory allocation and deallocation but also expose them to numerous pitfalls, such as memory leaks, dangling pointers, and buffer overflows. As applications grow in complexity, the task of ensuring correct memory usage becomes increasingly daunting. The consequences of mishandled memory can range from crashes to serious security vulnerabilities.

In contrast, garbage-collected languages like Java and Python simplify memory management, automatically reclaiming unused memory. However, this comes with its own trade-offs, including unpredictable performance and increased latency due to garbage collection. Rust stands out by offering memory safety guarantees without relying on garbage collection, instead employing an innovative ownership system.

5.2 Ownership and Borrowing

At the heart of Rust's memory management model is the concept of ownership, which governs how memory is accessed and managed. In Rust, every value has a single owner, which is typically a variable. The owner is responsible for the value's memory; when the owner goes out of scope, Rust automatically frees the associated memory. This model eliminates the need for manual memory management and significantly reduces the risk of memory leaks.

5.2.1 Ownership Rules

Rust's ownership system is governed by three primary rules:

Each value has a single owner at any given time.

When the owner of a value goes out of scope, Rust automatically deallocates the memory.

Ownership can be transferred (moved) but cannot be shared, ensuring that no two variables can simultaneously access the same memory location, preventing data races.

Example: Ownership in Action Consider the following Rust code snippet:

```rust
fn main() {

let s1 = String::from("Hello"); // s1 is the owner let s2 = s1; // Ownership is transferred to s2

// println!("{}", s1); // This will cause a compile-time error println!("{}", s2); // Works fine

}
```

In this example, `s1` initially owns the `String` value. When `s2` takes ownership of `s1`, the latter becomes invalid, preventing potential errors associated with accessing a freed resource.

5.2.2 Borrowing

While ownership in Rust restricts access to a single owner, the concept of borrowing allows temporary access without transferring ownership. Borrowing can be either mutable or immutable:

Immutable Borrowing: You can borrow a value multiple times as long as it remains immutable.

Mutable Borrowing: You can borrow a value once as mutable, but this disallows any other active borrows (mutable or immutable) at the same time.

This model facilitates safe concurrent access while preventing data races. #### Example: Borrowing in Action

```rust
fn main() {

let mut x = 5;

let y = &x; // Immutable borrow println!("y: {}", y);

let z = &mut x; // Mutable borrow

*z += 1; // Modify through mutable reference println!("x: {}", z);

}
```

In this example, `y` borrows `x` immutably, allowing

69

read access without modification. The mutable borrow

`z` allows the value of `x` to be changed, but no immutable borrow can exist simultaneously. ## 5.3 Lifetimes

While ownership and borrowing effectively manage memory, they can become complex when dealing with multiple references, leading to the introduction of lifetimes. Lifetimes ensure that references remain valid as long as the data they point to is accessible.

Rust uses lifetime annotations (e.g., `<'a>`) to specify how long references should be valid, helping the compiler verify that references neither outlive their data nor create dangling references.

Example: Lifetimes in Action

```rust
fn longest<'a>(s1: &'a str, s2: &'a str) -> &'a str { if s1.len() > s2.len() {

s1

} else { s2

}

}
```

In this example, the `longest` function returns a reference that is valid as long as the input references are valid. Rust leverages lifetimes to ensure memory safety at compile time.

5.4 Safety Guarantees

Rust's ownership and borrowing model, combined with lifetimes, provides strong safety guarantees:

Memory Safety: Rust enforces strict ownership rules that prevent dangling pointers and buffer overflows.

Thread Safety: By controlling mutable access and using ownership, Rust eliminates certain classes of data races at compile time, facilitating safe concurrency.

Compile-Time Checks: Many common memory-related bugs are caught during compilation, ensuring that the code is memory-safe before it even runs.

Memory management and safety are critical concerns in software development, and Rust's approach addresses these challenges with a robust and innovative design. The principles of ownership, borrowing, and lifetimes provide a framework that not only empowers developers with fine-grained control over memory but also guarantees safety without a garbage collector.

Understanding and harnessing Rust's memory management capabilities equips developers with the tools to build efficient, secure, and concurrent applications. In the subsequent chapters, we will delve into practical applications of these concepts, showcasing how Rust can be employed to build real-world systems with confidence.

How Rust Handles Memory Safely for IoT Applications

Within this context, the Rust programming language emerges as a powerful ally, offering a suite of features designed to prevent memory-related errors that can lead to vulnerabilities or system failures.

Understanding Memory Safety in IoT

Memory management is a fundamental concern in software development, particularly in resource-constrained environments like those typical of IoT devices. Traditional languages like C and C++ grant programmers fine-grained control over memory allocation and deallocation but come with inherent risks. Issues such as buffer overflows, null pointer dereferencing, and use-after-free errors can lead to crashes, unexpected behavior, or security loopholes that malicious actors can exploit.

In IoT applications, the stakes are elevated: a security breach could have dire consequences, ranging from data theft to physical damage. Additionally, the limited computing resources and power supply of many IoT devices necessitate efficient use of memory. Rust addresses these challenges with a unique approach to memory safety, aiming to minimize risk without compromising performance.

Rust's Ownership Model

At the heart of Rust's memory safety guarantees lies its ownership model. This innovative system operates on three core principles: ownership, borrowing, and lifetimes.

Ownership: Each piece of data in Rust has a single owner, which is responsible for managing its memory. When the owner goes out of scope, Rust automatically deallocates the memory, preventing memory leaks.

Borrowing: Rust allows references to data through

borrowing, which can be either mutable or immutable. This enables code to temporarily use data without assuming ownership, fostering collaboration among different components without risking inconsistencies.

Lifetimes: Rust employs lifetimes to track how long references to data are valid. This ensures that references do not outlive the data they point to, preventing dangling references and associated runtime errors.

By leveraging these concepts, developers can create IoT applications that are not only performant but also inherently safe from common memory issues. This is particularly critical in a landscape where updates may be scarce or challenging, necessitating an emphasis on building solid, resilient applications from the outset.

Performance Without Compromise

One of the primary benefits of Rust is its ability to provide memory safety without a garbage collector, which is often a source of unpredictability in terms of performance. In many IoT scenarios, especially those involving real-time processing, latency can lead to subpar user experiences or, worse, system failures.

Rust's zero-cost abstractions allow developers to write high-level code that compiles down to efficient machine code, meaning developers can focus on creating safe, concurrent, and performant applications without sacrificing responsiveness or efficiency. The language is designed to enable systems programming, which is essential for IoT devices that operate at the hardware level.

Concurrency and Safety

In an IoT ecosystem, devices often need to function concurrently, whether communicating with each other or processing multiple streams of data. Traditional threading models can introduce complexity and potential race conditions, making it difficult to manage shared resources. Rust's concurrency model offers safe concurrency by enforcing rules at compile time that prevent data races, ensuring that multiple threads can operate without stepping on each other's toes.

By utilizing Rust's concurrency features, developers can build scalable and responsive IoT applications that leverage parallelism while maintaining memory safety. This is vital for applications ranging from data collection in smart agriculture to real-time monitoring systems in industrial environments, where multiple devices must seamlessly work together.

Real-world Applications

Numerous IoT projects have successfully adopted Rust, showcasing its capabilities in the real world. For instance, smart sensors implementing edge computing can use Rust to process data locally, minimizing latency while ensuring that the devices remain secure against potential attacks. Additionally, in healthcare, where devices are critical for monitoring patient health, Rust offers the reliability required to handle sensitive data without the risk of memory corruption.

Rust's growing community and ecosystem also facilitate the development of IoT applications through libraries and frameworks specifically designed for low-level systems programming. Projects like `Tokio` for asynchronous programming, `Embedded Rust` for microcontroller development, and integrations with

`WebAssembly` enable a wide range of applications, from robust backend systems to resource-constrained firmware development.

As IoT continues to expand, the reliance on programming languages that prioritize robustness and security becomes indispensable. Rust stands out as a language that addresses the inherent challenges of memory management in IoT applications. Its ownership model, efficient performance, safe concurrency features, and an active community make it an ideal choice for developers aiming to craft reliable IoT systems.

Ownership, Borrowing, and Lifetimes in Embedded Rust

This chapter explores the concepts of ownership, borrowing, and lifetimes in the context of embedded Rust programming, shedding light on how these principles enhance safety and efficiency in resource-constrained environments.

Ownership in Rust

Ownership is a core concept of Rust's memory management model. It revolves around three main rules:

Each value in Rust has a single owner — a variable that is responsible for its memory.

When the owner goes out of scope, Rust automatically deallocates the associated memory.

Ownership can be transferred (moved) between variables.

In embedded systems, managing limited memory is crucial. Rust's ownership model assures developers that memory usage is precise: you can visually trace memory lifetimes through the ownership mechanism. For example, consider a simple embedded Rust program that manages a sensor reading:

```rust
struct Sensor { value: u32,
}

fn initialize_sensor() -> Sensor { Sensor { value: 0 }
}

fn update_sensor(sensor: Sensor) {
// sensor is now moved here; can't be used after this point
println!("Updating sensor: {}", sensor.value);
}

fn main() {
let sensor = initialize_sensor(); update_sensor(sensor);
// sensor can't be used here; it's been moved
}
```

In this example, when `sensor` is passed to `update_sensor`, ownership is transferred, preventing further use of the original `sensor` variable in `main`. This guarantees that there's no accidental usage of resources that may already have been cleaned up.

Borrowing

In embedded programming, data often requires concurrent access without transferring ownership. Rust provides borrowing as a solution, allowing functions to temporarily access resources without claiming ownership. Borrowing is represented as either mutable or immutable:

Immutable Borrowing: Multiple parts of the code can read data simultaneously without modifying it.

Mutable Borrowing: Only one borrow can exist at a time, ensuring exclusive access for modification. For example, consider the following code that demonstrates both types of borrowing:

```rust
fn read_sensor(sensor: &Sensor) { // immutable borrow
println!("Sensor value: {}", sensor.value);
}

fn update_sensor(sensor: &mut Sensor) { // mutable borrow sensor.value += 10;
}
fn main() {
let mut sensor = Sensor { value: 0 };


read_sensor(&sensor);      //    immutable    borrow
update_sensor(&mut sensor); // mutable borrow

}
```

In this example, `read_sensor` borrows `sensor` immutably, allowing multiple reads without locking the

77

resource. When `update_sensor` borrows `sensor` mutably, it ensures that no other parts of the program can access `sensor` until the mutable borrow ends. This ensures data integrity, a crucial aspect in real-time embedded systems.

Lifetimes

Lifetimes are a concept that helps the Rust compiler enforce the rules of borrowing. They ensure that references are always valid and do not outlive the data they point to. Lifetimes become especially valuable when dealing with complex structures and multiple borrows.

Rust uses lifetime annotations to indicate how long references should be valid:

```rust
struct SensorData<'a> { value: &'a u32,
}

fn process_sensor_data(sensor_data: SensorData) {
println!("Processing value: {}", sensor_data.value);
}
```

Here, the lifetime parameter `'a` specifies that the `value` reference within `SensorData` must not outlive the data it references. This guarantee prevents dangling pointers, a common pitfall in systems programming, particularly in embedded contexts where the timing of resource deletion can be unpredictable.

Practical Applications in Embedded Rust

The ownership, borrowing, and lifetime concepts play a

pivotal role in developing robust embedded systems. These features lead to:

Memory Safety: Preventing data races and dangling pointers ensures stability in performance-critical applications.

Predictability: With ownership rules delineating resource lifetimes, embedded systems can predict memory usage patterns and timing behavior.

Concurrency: Rust's borrowing system allows for safe concurrent operations, an essential requirement in many embedded applications.

As an illustration, consider an embedded application that manages an array of sensor readings and needs to process them in real time. By leveraging these concepts, it can safely update and read sensor data without the risks of corrupted states or accidental memory overwrites.

Ownership, borrowing, and lifetimes form the backbone of embedded Rust programming, offering developers tools to create safe, efficient, and predictable applications. In a domain where every byte of memory counts and safety is paramount, these features shine by eliminating common pitfalls associated with memory management.

Chapter 6: Sensor and Actuator Integration

In this chapter, we'll explore how to effectively communicate with sensors and actuators using Rust programming, highlighting libraries, best practices, and example projects.

Section 1: Understanding the Basics ### 1.1 What are Sensors and Actuators?

Sensors are devices that detect changes in the environment and convert them into data that can be processed. For example, temperature sensors measure ambient temperature, while motion sensors detect movement. On the other hand, actuators perform actions based on signals they receive. These can range from motors that control a robotic arm to relays that switch on lights.

1.2 The Role of Rust

Rust is designed to provide high performance with memory safety guarantees. This makes it an excellent choice for embedded systems where resources are limited, and reliability is paramount. Its concurrency model also allows efficient handling of multiple sensor inputs and actuator outputs, which is vital for real-time systems.

Section 2: Setting Up the Rust Environment ### 2.1 Installing Rust

To develop Rust applications, begin by installing Rust using `rustup`, which is the recommended way. Update your system's package manager or follow the instructions from the [official Rust website](https://www.rust-lang.org/tools/install).

```bash
curl --proto '=https' --tlsv1.2 -sSf https://sh.rustup.rs | sh
```

2.2 Cargo: The Rust Package Manager

Cargo is Rust's build system and package manager. It simplifies managing your projects and their dependencies. Create a new project using:

```bash
cargo new sensor_reader cd sensor_reader
```

Section 3: Interfacing with Sensors

3.1 Using I2C for Sensor Communication

Many sensors communicate over I2C (Inter-Integrated Circuit). Rust has several crates to facilitate I2C communication. One popular crate is `i2cdev`.

3.1.1 Adding Dependencies

Open `Cargo.toml` and include the `i2cdev` crate:

```toml
[dependencies]
i2cdev = "0.6" # Check for the latest version on crates.io
```

3.1.2 Reading Data from a Sensor

Below is a simple example of interfacing with a temperature sensor using I2C:

```rust
```

```
use i2cdev::core::I2CDevice;
use i2cdev::linux::LinuxI2CDevice; use std::error::Error;
fn read_temperature() -> Result<f32, Box<dyn Error>> {
let mut dev = LinuxI2CDevice::new("/dev/i2c-1", 0x48)?;
// Replace with your sensor's address let mut buffer = [0;
2];
dev.read(&mut buffer)?;
let temp = ((buffer[0] as u16) << 8 | buffer[1] as u16) >>
4;
Ok(temp as f32 * 0.0625) // Convert to Celsius based on
specific sensor's datasheet
}
fn main() {
match read_temperature() {
Ok(temp) => println!("Current temperature: {:.2}°C",
temp), Err(e) => println!("Error reading temperature: {}",
e),
}
}
```
```

## Section 4: Controlling Actuators

### 4.1 Using GPIO for Actuator Control

General Purpose Input/Output (GPIO) pins are often used to control actuators. The `rppal` crate is a great choice for interfacing with Raspberry Pi GPIO.

#### 4.1.1 Adding Dependencies Include `rppal` in your
```

`Cargo.toml` file:

```toml
[dependencies]
rppal = "0.12" # Check for the latest version on crates.io
```

4.1.2 Controlling an LED

Here's how to control an LED connected to a GPIO pin:

```rust
use rppal::gpio::Gpio;

use std::time::Duration; use std::thread;

fn main() {

let gpio = Gpio::new().unwrap();

let mut pin = gpio.get(18).unwrap().into_output(); // GPIO 18

loop {

pin.set_high();    thread::sleep(Duration::from_secs(1)); pin.set_low(); thread::sleep(Duration::from_secs(1));

}

}
```

Section 5: Best Practices for Integration ### 5.1 Safety and Error Handling

Safety is one of Rust's primary values. Always handle potential errors when reading from sensors and controlling actuators. Use Rust's `Result` type extensively to propagate errors and avoid panics.

5.2 Resource Management

Utilize Rust's ownership model to ensure that resources are cleaned up properly. When dealing with I2C devices or GPIO pins, make sure to release resources when they are no longer needed.

5.3 Logging and Monitoring

Integrating a logging framework, such as `log` with `env_logger`, can be incredibly helpful for debugging and monitoring the behavior of your system over time.

Section 6: Example Projects ### 6.1 Weather Station

A practical application could be a weather station that reads temperature and humidity from sensors and displays them on an LCD. This project will utilize both I2C for sensor communication and GPIO for control.

6.2 Home Automation System

Another interesting project is a home automation system that uses motion sensors to control lights. Here, you would integrate various sensors and actuators, managing them in a robust Rust application.

Integrating sensors and actuators in Rust programming opens up a world of possibilities for creating intelligent and responsive systems. Through the use of appropriate libraries and following best practices, developers can build reliable applications that leverage the unique strengths of Rust.

Reading Data from Sensors with Rust

Rust, a modern systems programming language, offers unique advantages in terms of safety, performance, and concurrency, making it an excellent choice for developing applications that interact with hardware components. In this chapter, we will explore how to read data from sensors using Rust, discussing key concepts, libraries, and practical examples.

Understanding Sensors and Their Role

Sensors are devices that detect events or changes in the environment and send the corresponding data to a processor. They can measure physical properties such as temperature, humidity, light, pressure, and many others. Examples of commonly used sensors include temperature sensors (like the DHT11), light sensors (like the photoresistor), and motion sensors (like the PIR sensor).

In embedded systems and IoT applications, reading data from sensors often requires interacting with hardware directly, which is where Rust's capabilities shine. Rust's strong guarantees about memory safety and data races make it an attractive option for systems programming.

Setting Up the Rust Environment

Before diving into sensor data reading, it's essential to set up your Rust environment. If you haven't already, install Rust through [rustup](https://rustup.rs/), which will manage Rust versions and associated tools easily:

```bash
curl --proto '=https' --tlsv1.2 -sSf https://sh.rustup.rs | sh
```

Once installed, you might want to set up your favorite text editor or IDE, such as Visual Studio Code or IntelliJ Rust.

Choosing the Right Hardware Interface

Sensors typically communicate with microcontrollers or computers using various interfaces such as:

GPIO (General-Purpose Input/Output): Used for simple digital sensors (on/off).

Analog Input: For sensors producing a variable voltage (e.g., potentiometers).

I2C (Inter-Integrated Circuit): A two-wire protocol for connecting multiple devices.

SPI (Serial Peripheral Interface): A higher-speed interface than I2C.

UART (Universal Asynchronous Receiver-Transmitter): For serial communication.

Based on the type of sensor you choose, you will need to select the corresponding interface and use Rust libraries that facilitate this communication.

Required Libraries and Dependencies

For interfacing with sensors in Rust, a common crate (Rust's term for a library) is `rppal`, which allows interaction with Raspberry Pi GPIO, I2C, and SPI. After setting up your project, include the `rppal` crate in your `Cargo.toml` file:

```toml
[dependencies]

rppal = "0.12.0"
```

Make sure to keep track of the latest version available on [crates.io](https://crates.io/crates/rppal). ## Example: Reading Temperature from a DHT11 Sensor

Let's walk through a practical example of reading temperature and humidity data from a DHT11 sensor using Rust. The DHT11 is a low-cost humidity and temperature sensor that communicates using a single wire protocol.

Wiring the DHT11 Sensor

Connect the sensor to a Raspberry Pi or any Linux-compatible device with GPIO pins:

VCC to 3.3V or 5V

GND to Ground

Data Pin to a GPIO pin (e.g., GPIO4) ### Writing the Rust Code

Create a new Rust project using Cargo:

```bash
cargo new dht11_sensor cd dht11_sensor
```

Edit the `src/main.rs` file as follows:

```rust
use rppal::gpio::{Gpio, OutputPin}; use rppal::i2c::I2c;

use std::{thread, time};

const GPIO_PIN: u8 = 4; // The GPIO pin we connected the DHT11 to fn main() {

let gpio = Gpio::new().expect("Failed to initialize GPIO");

let mut pin = gpio.get(GPIO_PIN).expect("Failed to get pin").into_output();

// Simulate sensor reading loop {
```

```
// DHT11 data reading logic will be placed here
// For the illustration, we assume that we receive
// arbitrary temperature and humidity data
let temperature = 22.5; // Simulated temperature let humidity = 45.0; // Simulated humidity
println!("Temperature:     {:.1}°C",     temperature); println!("Humidity: {:.1}%", humidity);
// Wait for 2 seconds before the next reading thread::sleep(time::Duration::from_secs(2));
}
}
```

Compiling and Running the Code Compile the program using Cargo:

```bash
cargo build
```

Then run the program:

```bash
cargo run
```

You will see simulated temperature and humidity readings printed every two seconds. ## Handling Errors

When dealing with hardware, it's essential to handle errors gracefully. Adjust the code above to include error handling as shown below:

```rust
```

```rust
fn main() {

let gpio = Gpio::new().expect("Failed to initialize GPIO");

let mut pin = gpio.get(GPIO_PIN).expect("Failed to get pin")
.into_output();

loop {

match read_dht11_data(&mut pin) { Ok((temperature, humidity)) => {

println!("Temperature:        {:.1}°C",        temperature);
println!("Humidity: {:.1}%", humidity);

}

Err(e) => eprintln!("Error reading DHT11: {:?}", e),

}

thread::sleep(time::Duration::from_secs(2));

}

}

fn    read_dht11_data(pin:    &mut    OutputPin)    ->
Result<(f32, f32), &'static str> {

// Implementation to read from DHT11 and return
temperature and humidity

// Return Ok or Err using the necessary logic

// Placeholder return Ok((22.5, 45.0))

}
```
```

By leveraging Rust's memory safety and concurrency
```

features, we can build robust applications that interact efficiently with the physical world. As you continue to experiment with different sensors and interfaces, you'll uncover the vast potential of combining Rust's programming capabilities with the world of IoT and embedded systems.

Controlling Actuators Efficiently in Rust programming

In the realm of embedded systems and robotics, actuators play a crucial role in bridging the gap between software and physical action. Actuators convert electrical signals into mechanical motion, enabling systems to perform a variety of tasks, from simple movements to complex interactions.

Understanding Actuators

Before delving into the control mechanisms, it's important to understand the types of actuators commonly used in embedded systems:

Electric Motors: These include DC motors, stepper motors, and servo motors. They are commonly used for precise movements.

Pneumatic Actuators: Often utilized in applications requiring high force with limited space, these actuators depend on compressed air.

Hydraulic Actuators: Used in heavy machinery, these actuators operate using liquid pressure.

Choosing the right actuator for your application involves considering factors such as power requirements, speed, torque, and control methods.

Setting Up Rust for Embedded Systems

Rust is well-suited for embedded programming due to its focus on safety and performance. To control actuators effectively, we need to set up the Rust toolchain for embedded development:

Install Rust: Follow the instructions on the [official Rust website](https://www.rust-lang.org/tools/install) to install the Rust toolchain.

Set Up `rustup` for Cross-Compilation: Since embedded systems often require cross-compilation, install the required target with:

```bash
rustup target add thumbv7em-none-eabi
```

Use `cargo` for Project Management: Create a new project specifically tailored for embedded systems:

```bash
cargo new actuator_control --bin cd actuator_control
```

Add Embedded Crates: Utilize crates such as `embedded-hal`, which provides traits for general embedded hardware access, or `riscv`, targeting specific architectures.

The Embedded Hardware Abstraction Layer (HAL)

The Embedded HAL is a crucial abstraction layer that standardizes hardware interactions. At its core, it defines traits for GPIO, PWM, I2C, SPI, and other interfaces necessary for interacting with hardware components, including actuators.

Here's a simple implementation using the embedded-hal crate:

```rust
use embedded_hal::pwm::{Pwm, Channel}; use embedded_hal::digital::v2::OutputPin; use embedded_hal::timer::CountDown;

struct Actuator<P, T> { pwm: P,

timer: T,

}

impl<P, T> Actuator<P, T> where

P: Pwm<Channel = impl OutputPin>, T: CountDown,

{

pub fn new(pwm: P, timer: T) -> Self { Actuator { pwm, timer }

}

pub fn move_actuator(&mut self, duty_cycle: f32) { if duty_cycle < 0.0 || duty_cycle > 1.0 {

panic!("Duty cycle must be between 0.0 and 1.0");

}

self.pwm.set_duty(duty_cycle);

}

pub fn wait(&mut self, duration: T::Time) { self.timer.start(duration);
```

```rust
        while self.timer.wait().is_ok() {}
    }
}
```

In this example, the `Actuator` struct encapsulates the logic for controlling an actuator using PWM. The

`move_actuator` method sets the PWM duty cycle, allowing control over the actuator's position or speed. ## Efficiently Controlling Actuators

1. Non-Blocking Control

In many scenarios, blocking operations can lead to inefficient use of CPU resources. Rust's concurrency model allows you to utilize asynchronous programming patterns to control actuators efficiently. Consider using the `async` and `await` features along with the `tokio` runtime to create asynchronous tasks for actuator control.

```rust
use tokio::time::{sleep, Duration};

async fn control_actuator_async(actuator: &mut Actuator, position: f32) {
    actuator.move_actuator(position);
    sleep(Duration::from_millis(100)).await; // Non-blocking wait
}
```

2. Utilizing Interrupts

For immediate and responsive control, consider using

hardware interrupts. By setting up interrupt handlers, you can react to events (e.g., reaching a certain position) without constantly polling the state of an actuator.

3. Implementing PID Control

For applications requiring precision, implementing a Proportional-Integral-Derivative (PID) controller can significantly enhance the performance of actuator control. The PID controller allows fine adjustments based on the difference between a desired setpoint and the actual position or condition of the actuator.

```rust
rust struct PID {

kp: f32, ki: f32, kd: f32,

integral: f32, previous_error: f32,

}

impl PID {

pub fn new(kp: f32, ki: f32, kd: f32) -> Self { PID {

kp,

ki,

kd,

integral: 0.0,

previous_error: 0.0,

}

}

pub fn compute(&mut self, setpoint: f32, measured: f32) -> f32 { let error = setpoint - measured;

self.integral += error;
```

```
let derivative = error - self.previous_error;

let output = self.kp * error + self.ki * self.integral + self.kd
* derivative; self.previous_error = error;

output
}
}
```
```

This PID controller can be integrated into your actuator control loop, enabling dynamic adjustment based on real-time feedback.

Efficient actuator control demands a thoughtful blend of hardware knowledge, programming skills, and the ability to use concurrent techniques. Rust, with its emphasis on safety and performance, presents a powerful foundational tool for building embedded systems that rely on actuators.
```

Chapter 7: Interfacing with IoT Communication Protocols

This chapter delves into the critical task of interfacing with IoT communication protocols in Rust, highlighting techniques, libraries, and best practices.

7.1 Overview of IoT Communication Protocols

Before diving into the practical aspects of Rust, it's essential to understand the common communication protocols used in IoT:

MQTT (Message Queuing Telemetry Transport): A lightweight protocol designed for low- bandwidth, high-latency environments. It operates on the publish-subscribe model, making it ideal for sending messages between devices.

CoAP (Constrained Application Protocol): Specifically tailored for use in constrained devices. CoAP is similar to HTTP but optimized for constrained networks, enabling devices to communicate using RESTful methods.

HTTP/HTTPS: The widely used HyperText Transfer Protocol can also be employed in IoT applications. However, its overhead makes it less suitable for constrained environments compared to MQTT or CoAP.

WebSocket: A protocol providing full-duplex communication channels over a single TCP connection. It is useful for real-time applications and scenarios requiring bidirectional communication.

LoRaWAN (Long Range Wide Area Network): A protocol primarily for low-power wide-area network applications. It excels in long-range communication with minimal power usage, making it suitable for remote sensors.

BLE (Bluetooth Low Energy): Commonly used for short-range low-power applications, it's popular in wearables and health-related IoT devices.

The choice of protocol significantly influences the design and functionality of IoT applications. ## 7.2 Setting Up the Rust Environment

To interface with these protocols, you'll first need to set up your Rust environment. The following steps ensure you have the necessary tools:

Install Rust: Follow the instructions at [rust-lang.org](https://www.rust-lang.org/tools/install) to install Rust and Cargo, Rust's package manager.

Set Up Your Project: Create a new Rust project using Cargo:

```bash
cargo new iot_interface cd iot_interface
```

Choose Protocol Libraries: Depending on the protocols you intend to work with, you will need various crates (Rust libraries). Some popular ones for IoT protocols include:

`rumqttc` for MQTT

`coap` for CoAP

`reqwest` for HTTP requests

`tokio-tungstenite` for WebSockets

You can add these dependencies to your `Cargo.toml` file:

```toml
[dependencies]
rumqttc = "0.5"

coap = "0.6"

reqwest = { version = "0.11", features = ["json"] }
tokio-tungstenite = "0.15"

tokio = { version = "1", features = ["full"] }
```

7.3 Interfacing with MQTT using Rust ### 7.3.1 Setting Up MQTT

MQTT is a popular protocol for IoT due to its lightweight nature. Here's how to set up a simple MQTT client:

```rust
use rumqttc::{MqttOptions, Client, Event, Notification};
use std::time::Duration;

fn main() {

// Create an MQTT client

let mut mqttoptions = MqttOptions::new("test_client", "broker.hivemq.com", 1883);
mqttoptions.set_keep_alive(Duration::from_secs(5));

let (mut client, mut connection) = Client::new(mqttoptions, 10);

// Subscribe to a topic client.subscribe("test/topic", 1).unwrap();

// Handle incoming messages loop {

for notification in connection.iter() { match notification {
```

98

```
Ok(Event::Incoming(Notification::Publish(p)))    =>    {
println!("Received: {:?}", p.payload);
}
Ok(_) => {}
Err(e) => println!("Error: {:?}", e),
}
}
}
}
```

7.3.2 Publishing Messages

You can publish messages to an MQTT topic:

```rust
let payload = "Hello, IoT!";

client.publish("test/topic",  rumqttc::QoS::AtLeastOnce,
false, payload).unwrap();
```

7.4 Interfacing with CoAP

CoAP allows constrained devices to communicate effectively. To set up a CoAP client, use the `coap` crate:

```rust
use coap::prelude::*;

fn main() {

let client = Client::new();
```

```rust
// Send a GET request
let response =
client.get("coap://example.com/resource").unwrap();
println!("Response: {}", response.payload);
}
```

7.5 Working with HTTP in Rust

HTTP remains a staple protocol. Using `reqwest`, you can build a simple HTTP client:

```rust
use reqwest;

#[tokio::main] async fn main() {

let response =
reqwest::get("https://api.example.com/data")

.await

.unwrap()

.text()

.await

.unwrap();

println!("Response: {}", response);

}
```

7.6 Securing IoT Communications

Security in IoT is of paramount importance. Here are some strategies for securing communications:

Use TLS/SSL: Ensure that communication over HTTP and MQTT is encrypted using TLS. The

`native-tls` crate can be integrated into your Rust application for this purpose.

Authentication Tokens: Implement token-based authentication to ensure that only authorized devices can communicate.

Data Validation: Always validate received data to protect against malicious payloads.

Regular Updates: Keep your libraries updated to mitigate vulnerabilities.

7.7 Best Practices

To ensure you develop effective IoT applications with Rust:

Modularity: Organize your code into modules for better maintainability.

Error Handling: Leverage Rust's robust error handling features to manage potential runtime errors.

Benchmarks and Tests: Regularly benchmark your communication routines to ensure they perform well under expected loads. Implement unit tests to guarantee the correctness of your code.

Choose the Right Protocol: Evaluate your application's requirements carefully before selecting a communication protocol.

This chapter has covered the fundamental aspects of interfacing with various IoT communication protocols in

Rust, providing a solid foundation for building IoT solutions. Moving forward, developers are encouraged to experiment with these examples and incorporate advanced features to enhance their Rust IoT applications further. The intersection of Rust and IoT presents a rich landscape of opportunities for innovation and efficiency.

Implementing Serial Communication (UART, SPI, I2C)

Serial communication protocols such as UART (Universal Asynchronous Receiver-Transmitter), SPI (Serial Peripheral Interface), and I2C (Inter-Integrated Circuit) are commonly used across various applications. This chapter focuses on implementing these protocols using the Rust programming language, highlighting their setup, benefits, and use cases.

5.1 Introduction to Serial Communication

Serial communication allows data to be sent one bit at a time over a communication channel. This is particularly advantageous in embedded systems, where resources are often limited. In this chapter, we'll explore the following protocols:

UART: A simple, asynchronous protocol used mainly for point-to-point communication.

SPI: A synchronous protocol ideal for high-speed communication between a master and one or more slaves.

I2C: A multi-master protocol that allows multiple devices to communicate over a two-wire connection.

5.2 Setting Up Rust for Embedded Development

Before implementing serial communication protocols, ensure your Rust environment is configured for embedded development. Follow these steps:

5.2.1 Install Rust

Make sure you have Rust installed on your system. You can install it using `rustup`:

```bash
curl --proto '=https' --tlsv1.2 -sSf https://sh.rustup.rs | sh
```

This command will download and install the Rust toolchain. ### 5.2.2 Set Up the Embedded Environment

To develop for embedded systems in Rust, you need the `Rust Embedded` ecosystem. Install the required tools:

```bash
rustup target add thumbv7em-none-eabi cargo install cargo-embed
```

Make sure you have an appropriate `Cargo.toml` file that includes necessary dependencies, such as

`embedded-hal` for hardware abstraction and `panic-halt` for error handling. ### 5.2.3 Choose a Board Support Package (BSP)

Select a BSP suitable for your microcontroller, such as `stm32f4`, `nrf51`, or `nrf52` crates. Add the appropriate dependencies to your `Cargo.toml`:

```toml
[dependencies]
embedded-hal = "0.2.6"

stm32f4xx-hal = "0.8.0"  # Example for STM32F4 series microcontroller
```

5.3 Implementing UART Communication ### 5.3.1 Overview of UART

UART is a widely used protocol for asynchronous communication. It requires only two wires: one for transmission (TX) and another for reception (RX).

5.3.2 Code Example

Here is a simple example of how to initialize and use UART on an STM32 microcontroller.

```rust
#![no_std] #![no_main]

use panic_halt as _; // panic handler use cortex_m_rt::entry;

use stm32f4xx_hal::{prelude::*, serial::{Serial, Config}};

#[entry]
fn main() -> ! {

let dp = stm32f4xx_hal::pac::Peripherals::take().unwrap(); let rcc = dp.RCC.constrain();

let clocks = rcc.cfgr.freeze(&dp.FLASH.constrain()); let gpioa = dp.GPIOA.split();

// Initialize UART

let tx = gpioa.pa2.into_alternate_af7(); let rx =
```

```
gpioa.pa3.into_alternate_af7();
```

let serial = Serial::usart2(dp.USART2, (tx, rx), Config::default(), clocks).unwrap(); loop {

let byte = serial.read().unwrap(); // Wait for a byte to arrive

serial.bwrite_all(&[byte]).unwrap(); // Echo the received byte

```
}
}
```
```

### 5.3.3 Explanation

**Setup**: The code initializes the USART peripheral, configuring the TX and RX pins.

**Communication Loop**: Inside the loop, the program waits for a byte to be received and immediately echoes it back.

## 5.4 Implementing SPI Communication ### 5.4.1 Overview of SPI

SPI is a high-speed, synchronous protocol that requires four signal lines: MOSI (Master Out Slave In), MISO (Master In Slave Out), SCK (Serial Clock), and SS (Slave Select).

### 5.4.2 Code Example

Here's how you can set up SPI communication:

```rust
use stm32f4xx_hal::{spi::Spi, spi::Mode, prelude::*};
```
```

```rust
fn setup_spi() -> Spi<pac::SPI1, (Pins), Mode> { let gpioa
= dp.GPIOA.split();

let gpioa_pins = ( gpioa.pa5.into_alternate_af5(), // SCK
gpioa.pa6.into_alternate_af5(),            //          MISO
gpioa.pa7.into_alternate_af5(), // MOSI
);

let spi = Spi::spi1(dp.SPI1, gpioa_pins, Mode::new(),
1.mhz(), clocks, &mut rcc.apb2).unwrap(); spi
}

fn perform_spi_transfer(spi: &mut Spi<pac::SPI1, (Pins),
Mode>) { let data: u8 = 0x55; // Example data

let response = spi.transfer(&mut data).unwrap(); // Read
response from SPI device
}
```

5.4.3 Explanation

Initialization: The SPI peripheral is initialized, specifying the mode of operation and speed.

Data Transfer: The transfer function sends data and retrieves the response in a single method call. ## 5.5 Implementing I2C Communication

5.5.1 Overview of I2C

I2C is a two-wire protocol allowing for multiple devices to communicate on the same bus. It uses SDA (Serial Data Line) and SCL (Serial Clock Line) for communication.

5.5.2 Code Example

Here's a concise example to set up and communicate via I2C:

```rust
use stm32f4xx_hal::{i2c::I2c, i2c::Mode, prelude::*};

fn setup_i2c() -> I2c<pac::I2C1, (Sda, Scl), Mode> { let gpiob = dp.GPIOB.split();

let sda = gpiob.pb7.into_alternate_open_drain(); let scl = gpiob.pb6.into_alternate_open_drain();

I2c::i2c1(dp.I2C1, (sda, scl), 100.khz(), clocks, &mut rcc.apb1)
}

fn perform_i2c_transfer(i2c: &mut I2c<pac::I2C1, (Sda, Scl), Mode>, address: u16) { let data: [u8; 2] = [0x00, 0x01]; // Example data

i2c.write(address, &data).unwrap(); // Send data

}
```

5.5.3 Explanation

I2C Setup: The I2C peripheral is initialized, specifying the SDA and SCL pins.

Data Transmission: The write method sends data to a specified I2C address.

In this chapter, we explored three crucial serial communication protocols: UART, SPI, and I2C. We highlighted their setups and provided practical Rust code examples for each protocol. Rust, with its safety guarantees and performance, is an excellent choice for embedded system programming, effectively bringing robust serial communication to your projects.

Networking IoT Devices with MQTT

This protocol is especially suited for IoT applications due to its low bandwidth requirements and publish/subscribe architecture. We will also leverage Rust, a systems programming language known for its performance and safety features, to implement our MQTT solutions.

What is MQTT?

MQTT operates on a client-server architecture where clients publish messages to a broker, which then distributes these messages to subscribers that have expressed interest in a particular topic. The key features of MQTT include:

Lightweight Protocol: MQTT uses minimal bandwidth, making it ideal for IoT devices that often operate in constrained environments.

Publish/Subscribe Mechanism: This decouples the producers of data (publishers) from consumers (subscribers), facilitating scalability and flexibility.

Quality of Service Levels: MQTT defines three QoS levels (0, 1, 2) that allow developers to choose the message delivery assurance that fits their application needs.

Retained Messages: The broker can store the last message sent on a topic, allowing new subscribers to immediately receive the most recent state.

Why Use Rust for IoT?

Rust's strong emphasis on safety and concurrency makes it an excellent choice for developing IoT applications. Key advantages include:

Memory Safety: Rust's ownership model prevents common bugs such as null pointer dereferences and buffer overflows, ensuring that IoT devices can run reliably in production.

Performance: Rust compiles to native code, providing performance comparable to C/C++ while maintaining higher safety guarantees.

Concurrency: Rust's concurrency model allows developers to write multithreaded applications without fear of data races, a common challenge in IoT systems.

Getting Started with Rust and MQTT ### Setting Up the Environment

To get started, ensure you have Rust installed. If you haven't installed it yet, you can do so by following the instructions on the official [Rust website](https://www.rust-lang.org/tools/install). After the installation, create a new Rust project:

```bash
cargo new mqtt_iot cd mqtt_iot
```

Adding Dependencies

We will use the `rumqttc` library, a Rust MQTT client that provides support for the MQTT protocol. To add it to your project, modify the `Cargo.toml` file:

```toml [dependencies]
rumqttc = "0.9" # Check for the latest version on crates.io
tokio = { version = "1", features = ["full"] }
```

Implementing an MQTT Client

Now that we have our dependencies in place, let's implement a simple MQTT client that can connect to a broker, publish a message, and subscribe to a topic.

Main Code Structure

The main structure of our code will include creating a client, connecting to the broker, publishing a message, and subscribing to a topic for messages.

```rust
use rumqttc::{MqttOptions, Client, QoS, Event, Notification, AsyncClient}; use std::time::Duration;

use tokio::runtime::Runtime;

#[tokio::main] async fn main() {

// Set up MQTT options

let mut mqttoptions = MqttOptions::new("mqtt_iot_client", "broker.hivemq.com", 1883); mqttoptions.set_keep_alive(Duration::from_secs(5));

// Create a client

let (mut client, mut connection) =
```

```rust
Client::new(mqttoptions, 10);
// Launch a connection loop tokio::spawn(async move {
for notification in connection.iter() { match notification {
Ok(Event::Incoming(Notification::Message(msg))) => {
println!("Received message on topic {}: {:?}", msg.topic,
msg.payload);
},
Ok(Event::Incoming(Notification::Other)) => {
// Handle other notifications (if needed)
},
Err(e) => {
eprintln!("Error during MQTT connection: {:?}", e);
}
}
});
}
_ => {}
```

```rust
// Subscribe to a topic
client.subscribe("home/temperature",
QoS::AtLeastOnce).unwrap();
// Publish a message
let payload = "Current temperature is 24 degrees
Celsius.";           client.publish("home/temperature",
QoS::AtLeastOnce, false, payload).unwrap();
```

```
}
```

Explanation of Code

Set Up MQTT Options: We define the MQTT options, including the client ID, broker address (in this case, we are using a public broker for demonstration), and keep-alive duration.

Create a Client: The `Client::new()` function sets up the MQTT client and initiates communication with the broker.

Connection Loop: We spawn an asynchronous task to listen for incoming messages. The client will print any messages it receives on the specified topic.

Subscribing and Publishing Messages: The `subscribe` method allows the client to listen for messages under a specific topic, while the `publish` method sends a message to that topic.

Testing the Implementation

To test the implementation, make sure your MQTT broker is running and execute the Rust application:

```bash
cargo run
```

You should see any messages published to the `home/temperature` topic print out in your terminal.

In this chapter, we explored how to effectively use MQTT for networking IoT devices with the Rust programming language. We learned about the MQTT protocol's fundamental aspects and implemented a simple MQTT client that can publish and subscribe to messages. Rust's strong safety features and performance metrics position it as an excellent choice for IoT applications in a world increasingly dependent on connected devices.

Chapter 8: Building Secure IoT Applications with Rust

We will start with an overview of the core principles of IoT security, followed by a discussion on Rust features that lend themselves to safer programming practices, and conclude with practical examples and guidelines for building your own IoT applications.

8.1 Understanding IoT Security Challenges

Before diving into IoT application development, it is essential to understand the security challenges posed by IoT devices. These challenges include:

Limited Resources: Many IoT devices have constrained processing power, memory, and battery life. This can lead to the use of lightweight protocols and reduced security measures.

Diverse Ecosystem: IoT devices come with various hardware and software configurations, leading to inconsistencies in security approaches and vulnerabilities.

Interconnectivity: The interdependent nature of IoT systems means that a vulnerability in one device could potentially compromise an entire network.

Data Integrity and Privacy: IoT devices often collect sensitive data, raising concerns regarding confidentiality and proper data handling techniques.

Given these challenges, designing IoT applications with security in mind from the ground up is imperative. ## 8.2 Why Choose Rust for IoT Development?

Rust offers unique features that make it well-suited for

developing secure IoT applications:

Memory Safety: Rust's ownership model enforces strict borrowing rules, ensuring memory safety and preventing common vulnerabilities such as buffer overflows or use-after-free errors.

Concurrency: With Rust's concurrency model, developers can harness multi-threading without the typical pitfalls associated with race conditions, making it easier to write efficient and safe concurrent code.

Performance: Rust provides low-level control akin to C/C++ without sacrificing performance, making it ideal for resource-constrained IoT devices.

Ecosystem: The rapidly growing Rust ecosystem features libraries and frameworks tailored to IoT, enhancing productivity and ensuring best practices.

8.3 Setting Up the Rust Environment for IoT Development

Before writing code, we need to set up our development environment. Here's a quick guide to get you started:

Install Rust: Use [rustup](https://rustup.rs/) for an easy installation of Rust and its toolchain.

```bash
curl --proto '=https' --tlsv1.2 -sSf https://sh.rustup.rs | sh
```

Set Up Cargo: Cargo is Rust's package manager and build system. It is essential for managing dependencies and simplifying the build process.

115

Select an Appropriate Target: For IoT, you may need to target embedded systems. You can set up a specific target by installing the required toolchain:

```bash
rustup target add thumbv7em-none-eabi
```

Choose Dependencies: Familiarize yourself with crates (Rust libraries) relevant to IoT, such as `rust-lang/embedded`, `tokio`, and `serde`.

8.4 Developing a Secure IoT Application

Now that we've set up our environment, let's walk through a simple example of building a secure IoT application using Rust.

Example: Temperature Sensor

In this example, we will create a temperature sensor application that reads data from a temperature sensor, securely sends data over a network, and uses encryption.

Step 1: Define the Sensor Structure

We start by defining a structure to represent our sensor:

```rust
#[derive(serde::Serialize, serde::Deserialize)] struct TemperatureSensor {

id: String, temperature: f32,

}
```

Step 2: Reading Sensor Data

This function simulates reading data from the sensor:

```rust
fn read_temperature() -> TemperatureSensor { let sensor
= TemperatureSensor {

id: "sensor_001".to_string(),

temperature: 22.5, // Simulated temperature

};

sensor

}
```

Step 3: Secure Data Transmission

We can use the `aes` crate to encrypt the sensor data before sending it:

```rust
use aes::Aes128;

use cipher::{NewBlockCipher, BlockDecrypt,
BlockEncrypt, KeyInit};


fn encrypt_data(sensor: &TemperatureSensor,
encryption_key: &[u8; 16]) -> Vec<u8> { let plaintext =
serde_json::to_vec(sensor).unwrap();

let mut cipher =
Aes128::new(KeyInit::new(encryption_key)); let mut
block = plaintext.clone();

cipher.encrypt_block(&mut block);
```

block

}

```

#### Step 4: Simulating Data Transmission

For demonstration purposes, we will print the encrypted data instead of sending it over a network.

```rust
fn main() {

let encryption_key = b"an example key 1"; // 16-byte key for AES-128 let sensor_data = read_temperature();

let encrypted_data = encrypt_data(&sensor_data, encryption_key);


println!("Encrypted Temperature Data: {:?}", encrypted_data);

}
```

Step 5: Enhancing Security

Additional security enhancements to consider for IoT applications include:

Secure Boot: Ensure that only trusted firmware can run on the device.

Firmware Updates: Implement secure mechanisms for updating firmware to patch vulnerabilities or improve functionality.

Authentication: Use secure authentication methods
```

(e.g., OAuth, JWT) to assert the identities of devices and users interacting with the IoT system.

By leveraging Rust's advantages, developers can create applications that not only deliver functionality but are also resilient against the myriad of security threats in today's interconnected landscape. As the IoT continues to grow, the ability to build secure, efficient applications will be paramount to safeguarding our digital and physical worlds. As you embark on your IoT journey with Rust, remember to always prioritize security at every stage of development.

Cryptographic Libraries and Secure Communication

In this chapter, we will explore the landscape of cryptographic libraries available in Rust, best practices for implementing secure communication, and practical examples to illustrate these concepts.

Understanding Cryptography

Cryptography is the science of securing communication and information through the use of mathematical techniques. It ensures the confidentiality, integrity, and authenticity of data. Essential cryptographic concepts include:

Symmetric Encryption: The same key is used for both encryption and decryption. Algorithms such as AES (Advanced Encryption Standard) fall under this category.

Asymmetric Encryption: Uses a pair of keys—a public

key for encryption and a private key for decryption. RSA (Rivest-Shamir-Adleman) is a prominent asymmetric algorithm.

Hash Functions: These are one-way functions that transform data into a fixed-length string, used for ensuring data integrity. Common hashing algorithms include SHA-256 and SHA-3.

Digital Signatures: These provide authenticity and non-repudiation, ensuring that a message has been sent by a recognized source.

Cryptographic Libraries in Rust

Rust boasts a number of libraries that provide cryptographic functionalities, each with different levels of abstraction and features catering to various needs. Some of the most prominent ones include:

1. **RustCrypto**

The RustCrypto project is a collection of cryptographic algorithms implented in Rust. This project is modular, meaning developers can use only the parts they need. The library includes implementations for hashing (e.g., SHA-1, SHA-256), asymmetric cryptography (RSA, Ed25519), and symmetric encryption (AES).

```toml
[dependencies] aes = "0.7.5"

sha2 = "0.10.5"

rsa = "0.5.0"

ed25519-dalek = "1.0.0"
```

2. **Ring**

The Ring library is designed for performance and ease of use, focusing on secure algorithms and avoiding pitfalls of low-level programming. It provides support for elliptic curves, hashing, and various secure protocols. It is suitable for applications requiring high-speed cryptographic operations.

```toml
[dependencies]
ring = "0.16"
```

3. **Sodiumoxide**

Sodiumoxide is a Rust binding to the Libsodium library, which is renowned for its simplicity and security. It serves as an effective alternative for cryptographic operations such as secret-key encryption, public-key authentication, and digital signatures.

```toml
[dependencies]
sodiumoxide = { version = "0.2", features = ["all"] }
```

4. **OpenSSL**

For projects that require interoperability with existing infrastructure or need specific OpenSSL features, the

`openssl` crate provides a Rust interface to the OpenSSL library. However, developers should be wary of the complexities and potential issues around memory management.

```toml
[dependencies]
openssl = "0.10"
```

121

Implementing Secure Communication

When implementing secure communication using Rust, there are essential protocols and practices developers should consider:

Securing Data Transmission

Transport Layer Security (TLS): Use the `rustls` or `native-tls` libraries for secure transport of data over networks. TLS is the cornerstone of secure communication on the internet.

Sample Implementation of a Secure TCP Client

Here's a simplified example of using `rustls` to establish a secure communication channel between a client and server.

Add Dependencies:

```toml
[dependencies]
rustls = "0.20"
tokio = { version = "1", features = ["full"] }
```

Client Code:

```rust
use std::sync::Arc;

use tokio::net::TcpStream;

use rustls::{ClientConfig, ClientSession, Stream}; use std::io::{self, Write, Read};

async fn connect_to_server(domain: &str, addr: &str) -> io::Result<()> { let mut config = ClientConfig::new(); config.set_root_certificates(rustls::RootCertStore::new());
```

```
let arc_config = Arc::new(config);

let stream = TcpStream::connect(addr).await?;

let mut session = ClientSession::new(&arc_config,
domain); let mut stream = Stream::new(&mut session,
stream);

// The application data to send

let data = b"Hello, secure server!";


// Send data stream.write_all(data).await?; Ok(())

}
```
```

## Best Practices for Cryptography in Rust

**Use Established Libraries**: When working with
cryptographic functions, it's crucial to rely on well-
established libraries instead of implementing your own.
Established libraries have undergone rigorous testing and
peer review.

**Regularly Update Dependencies**: Cryptography is a
rapidly evolving field, and vulnerabilities are regularly
discovered in cryptographic algorithms. Keeping
dependencies updated helps in mitigating risks.

**Avoid Low-Level Cryptography**: Use high-level
abstractions provided by libraries, such as

`rustcrypto` or `ring`, which handle many of the
common pitfalls of cryptographic operations.

**Always Validate Inputs**: Implement comprehensive
input validation to protect against common attacks, such
```

as buffer overflows and injection attacks.

Educate Yourself: Cryptography is complex. Take time to understand the cryptographic principles behind the libraries you choose, and stay updated with the latest developments and threats in the field.

By adhering to best practices and leveraging established libraries, developers can build highly secure applications that stand the test of time against potential vulnerabilities. As we advance, the importance of cryptography will only increase, making it a vital area of focus for all developers in the tech landscape.

Strategies to Protect IoT Devices from Cyber Threats

IoT devices are often vulnerable targets for cyber threats due to their diverse operating environments, limited computing resources, and often inadequate security implementations. In this chapter, we will explore effective strategies for protecting IoT devices from cyber threats, particularly within the context of programming in Rust. Rust, with its emphasis on safety and performance, provides unique features that can bolster IoT security.

Understanding IoT Vulnerabilities

Before delving into protective strategies, it is essential to understand the common vulnerabilities inherent in IoT devices:

Weak Authentication: Many IoT devices use default passwords or weak authentication mechanisms, making them easy targets for unauthorized access.

Unpatched Software: IoT devices often operate on outdated firmware due to the challenges of updating vast numbers of distributed devices.

Insecure Communication: Data transmitted without encryption can be intercepted, leading to data breaches or device manipulation.

Lack of Physical Security: Many IoT devices are deployed in unsecured environments, making them susceptible to physical tampering and theft.

Resource Limitations: IoT devices typically have limited processing power and memory, which can constrain their ability to implement robust security measures.

Given these vulnerabilities, applying appropriate security strategies is crucial. Below, we outline several strategies that leverage Rust's strengths to enhance IoT security.

1. Employing Strong Authentication Mechanisms

User authentication is the first line of defense against unauthorized access. IoT devices should implement:

Public Key Infrastructure (PKI): Leverage Rust crates such as `rustls` for implementing secure TLS communications, which can utilize certificates for strong, identity-based authentication.

Multi-Factor Authentication: While limited by resources, simple multi-factor authentication methods, such as PINs or physical tokens, can add an extra layer of security.

Secure Credential Storage: Rust's ownership model

125

and memory safety features can help securely store sensitive credentials using libraries like `secrecy` to ensure that credentials are not inadvertently exposed.

2. Utilizing Secure Communication Protocols

Data transmitted between IoT devices and servers must be protected from eavesdropping and tampering:

Encryption: Use robust encryption protocols such as AES for data at rest and TLS for data in transit. Rust's `aes` and `ring` crates can help implement these cryptographic protocols efficiently.

Secure Boot Processes: Implement secure boot mechanisms to ensure that only authorized firmware can run on the device, using Rust's capability to create trusted binaries.

Data Integrity Schemes: Implement cryptographic checksums or hash functions (e.g., using `sha2`) to verify the integrity of the data being transmitted.

3. Regular Firmware Updates

Keeping firmware up-to-date is critical for patching vulnerabilities:

Automated Update Mechanisms: Build an automated update system that securely downloads and installs updates. Rust's package manager, Cargo, can help manage dependencies and ensure that components are updated.

Checksum Verification: Utilize checksums to verify the authenticity and integrity of updates before installation, ensuring that the firmware has not been tampered with.

4. Monitoring and Logging

Continuous monitoring can help detect and respond to threats in real-time:

Event Logging: Implement systematic logging of device events and interactions. Rust's built-in `log` crate can facilitate efficient logging practices.

Anomaly Detection: Use Rust's performance capabilities to analyze logs and detect anomalies or suspicious behavior quickly, leveraging algorithms suited for resource-constrained environments.

5. Implementing Defense in Depth

A multi-layered security approach helps mitigate vulnerabilities:

Sandboxes and Containers: Utilize sandboxing techniques to isolate critical processes and mitigate the impact of a potential compromise.

Diverse Security Mechanisms: Combine various security techniques, such as firewalls, intrusion detection systems, and anomaly detection, to create redundancy in security layers.

6. Leveraging Community and Industry Standards
Utilizing established standards can enhance security:

Adhere to Security Frameworks: Follow IoT security frameworks such as the OWASP IoT Top Ten to understand common pitfalls and recommended practices.

Join Security Communities: Engaging with security communities can help stay informed about the latest threats and countermeasures relevant to IoT devices.

By employing strong authentication, secure communication protocols, and continuous monitoring, along with a commitment to regular updates and adherence to best practices, we can create a more secure IoT landscape. The future of IoT security lies in our collective commitment to implementing these strategies and continuously evolving them in response to emerging threats.

Chapter 9: Real-Time Programming in Rust

In this chapter, we will explore Rust's capabilities for real-time programming, focusing on its concurrency model, memory management, and tooling that aid in developing low-latency applications.

9.1 Understanding Real-Time Systems

In designing real-time systems, it is essential to differentiate between hard and soft real-time systems:

Hard Real-Time Systems: In these systems, failing to meet deadlines could result in catastrophic failures. Examples include pacemakers, automotive safety systems, and flight control systems.

Soft Real-Time Systems: These systems aim to meet deadlines, but occasional deadline misses are tolerable without severe consequences. Media streaming and online gaming are prime examples.

Real-time applications often require features like multitasking, priority scheduling, and predictable memory usage. Rust's community and ecosystem provide powerful abstractions and tools to cater to these requirements.

9.2 Rust's Concurrency Model

One of the cornerstones of real-time programming is the efficient management of concurrency. Rust offers a unique take on concurrency through its ownership model, which prevents data races at compile time. This feature is particularly advantageous for real-time programming, where unpredictable runtime behavior can be detrimental.

9.2.1 Ownership and Borrowing

In Rust, the ownership rules enable safe memory access without needing a garbage collector. This is crucial for real-time systems where you need predictable performance. By enforcing static memory safety checks, developers can be assured that data cannot be modified unexpectedly, which is essential in environments where timing is critical.

9.2.2 Lightweight Threads

Rust's threading model supports lightweight threads called "tasks." The `async` and `await` keywords enable writing asynchronous code that looks synchronous, simplifying the development of concurrent applications. This functionality is vital for real-time systems that need to handle multiple operations simultaneously while maintaining responsiveness.

9.3 Real-Time Libraries and Frameworks

Rust's ecosystem includes several libraries and frameworks specifically designed to facilitate real-time programming.

9.3.1 RTIC (Real-Time Interrupt-driven Concurrency)

RTIC is a framework for building real-time applications on embedded systems. It allows developers to create applications that can handle interrupts safely and efficiently. With RTIC, tasks can be prioritized, and the framework guarantees deterministic behavior in response to events, making it an excellent choice for hard real-time applications.

9.3.2 Tokio

While Tokio is primarily known for building asynchronous applications, it can also be utilized in real-time systems where soft real-time requirements exist. It provides utilities for managing timers, and scheduling tasks with varying priorities. Care should be taken, however, to manage latency and ensure appropriate task prioritization to meet the requirements of the specific application.

9.4 Performance Optimization Techniques

In real-time systems, every microsecond counts, and Rust provides several patterns and techniques to optimize performance further.

9.4.1 Memory Allocation Strategies

Inefficient memory allocation can lead to unpredictable latency. Rust's ownership model encourages stack allocation and the use of `Box`, `Rc`, and `Arc` for heap allocation with controlled lifetime. Using `no_std` for embedded programming can also help to fine-tune the memory usage, as it removes unnecessary components not suitable for real-time environments.

9.4.2 Lock-Free Programming

Rust's concurrency primitives allow for lock-free programming techniques, which can be essential in systems where lock contention leads to latency. Using atomic types and custom data structures, developers can avoid the pitfalls associated with traditional locking mechanisms.

9.5 Tooling and Analysis

Tools play a significant role in the development of real-time applications. Rust's tooling ecosystem includes various analysis tools that can help ensure your system meets its timing requirements.

9.5.1 Profiling and Benchmarking

Tools such as `cargo bench` and `flamegraph` provide insights into performance bottlenecks and allow developers to profile their applications, ensuring they meet real-time constraints. Benchmarking critical sections of code can inform design decisions and help tighten response times.

9.5.2 Static Analysis

Tools like Clippy and `rust-analyzer` offer insights into potential violations of Rust's ownership and borrowing rules. While these tools focus primarily on code quality and safety, they also contribute to predictable behavior, an essential quality in real-time systems.

9.6 Case Studies

To understand the practical implications of real-time programming in Rust, examining case studies of successful real-time applications can be helpful:

Embedded Systems: A generic microcontroller application developed using RTIC to manage multiple sensor inputs while guaranteeing response times within strict constraints.

Robotic Control Systems: A Rust-based control system for a robotic arm that uses asynchronous programming to manage real-time position feedback while maintaining the ability to respond instantly to changes in sensor data.

Introduction to Real-Time Operating Systems (RTOS)

Unlike general-purpose operating systems, RTOS are designed for predictability and reliability, ensuring that tasks get executed within specified time constraints (determinism).

1.1.1 Types of Real-Time Systems

RTOS can generally be categorized into two main types based on their timing constraints:

Hard Real-Time Systems: These systems require strict deadlines, where missing a deadline could lead to catastrophic failures. Examples include medical devices, aerospace systems, and industrial automation systems.

Soft Real-Time Systems: These systems can tolerate occasional deadline misses. While efficiency and response time are important, the system can still function correctly even if tasks are delayed. Examples include video streaming and online gaming.

1.1.2 Key Features of RTOS

RTOS have several defining characteristics, including:

Deterministic Behavior: Ability to predict the execution time of tasks and provide guaranteed response times.

Multitasking: Capability to manage multiple tasks or threads, allowing for parallel processing in a controlled manner.

Priority Scheduling: Tasks are given priorities; higher-priority tasks preempt lower-priority ones to ensure critical tasks meet their deadlines.

Inter-task Communication: Mechanisms are in place for tasks to communicate with each other safely and efficiently.

Minimal Latency: Quick response to external events, minimizing the wait time for task execution. ## 1.2 Why Use Rust for RTOS Development?

Rust is a modern programming language known for its performance, memory safety, and concurrency features, making it an excellent choice for developing real-time systems. Its unique characteristics address some of the common challenges faced in embedded and real-time systems, providing both safety and efficiency.

1.2.1 Key Advantages of Rust

Memory Safety: Rust's ownership system prevents common memory-related bugs, such as null pointer dereferences or buffer overflows, which are particularly critical in real-time applications.

Concurrency without Data Races: Rust's type system enforces thread safety at compile time, allowing developers to create concurrent applications that avoid data races, a common pitfall in multi-threaded programming.

Performance: Rust compiles to native machine code, resulting in efficient execution time suitable for resource-constrained environments typical in RTOS.

Zero-Cost Abstractions: Rust allows for high-level abstractions without incurring runtime overhead, enabling developers to write cleaner, more manageable code without sacrificing performance.

Embedded Ecosystem: Rust has a growing ecosystem of libraries and frameworks specifically designed for embedded and real-time systems, making it easier to build and maintain RTOS applications.

1.3 The Rust Ecosystem for RTOS

Rust provides a variety of libraries and tools tailored for developing RTOS applications. These include: ### 1.3.1 No-Standard-Library (no_std) Support

Rust's `no_std` environment is ideal for embedded programming, allowing developers to build applications without relying on the standard library. This is particularly important for RTOS, where minimizing footprint and dependency on system resources is crucial.

1.3.2 Embedded Frameworks

Several frameworks such as **RTIC (Real-Time Interrupt-driven Concurrency)** and **embassy** offer abstractions and utilities for prioritizing tasks, managing interrupts, and handling safe concurrent execution, all of which cater specifically to real-time applications.

1.3.3 Tools for Development

Rust's tooling, such as `cargo` for dependency management and building, along with testing frameworks, facilitates rapid development and ensures reliability in the code. The Rust community is active in creating tools and libraries geared towards the challenges of RTOS development.

1.4 Getting Started with Rust and RTOS

As you embark on developing with Rust for real-time
135

systems, you should set up your development environment, choose an appropriate Rust RTOS framework, and familiarize yourself with safety patterns and concurrency models unique to Rust.

1.4.1 Setting Up

Install Rust: Use `rustup` to install the latest stable version of Rust.

Configure for Embedded Development: Add the necessary targets for your microcontroller or embedded platform.

Select an RTOS Framework: Consider using RTIC or another suitable framework, depending on your project requirements.

1.4.2 Practical Exercises

Start with simple projects to get familiarized with Rust syntax, error handling, and concurrency patterns. Gradually move on to implement simple RTOS features, such as task scheduling and inter-task communication, ensuring to leverage the Rust guarantees of safety and efficiency.

The integration of Rust into the realm of Real-Time Operating Systems opens new horizons for developers seeking to build reliable, efficient, and safe applications. With memory safety features, performance capabilities, and growing community support, Rust represents a compelling choice for modern RTOS development.

Writing Real-Time Applications with Rust

These systems require timely execution of tasks with predictable behavior, often under stringent resource constraints. Rust, a programming language known for its performance, safety, and concurrency, has emerged as a popular choice for developing real-time applications. This chapter will explore the concepts, structures, and techniques for writing real-time applications using Rust.

Understanding Real-Time Systems

Before diving into Rust, it's crucial to understand what a real-time system is. Real-time systems are designed to operate within strict time constraints. They can be divided into two main categories:

Hard Real-Time Systems: These systems must meet their deadlines; failure to do so can lead to catastrophic outcomes. Examples include flight control systems and medical devices.

Soft Real-Time Systems: These systems can tolerate some missed deadlines, but performance degrades with increased latency. Multimedia applications and online transaction systems fit into this category.

In either case, Rust's features make it an excellent candidate for real-time systems development. ## Why Choose Rust for Real-Time Applications?

Rust provides several advantages that align well with the needs of real-time systems:

Memory Safety: Rust's ownership model eliminates data races at compile time, allowing developers to write concurrent code without fear of undefined behavior.

Performance: Rust compiles to native code, ensuring fast execution and minimal overhead, which are crucial for time-sensitive applications.

Concurrency Support: Rust's concurrency primitives and its actor model aid in building systems that efficiently manage multiple tasks simultaneously.

Low-level Control: Rust allows for fine-grained control over system resources, which is essential for meeting the stringent requirements of real-time applications.

Cross-platform Capabilities: Rust's ability to compile to different platforms easily accommodates a wide array of hardware, making it ideal for embedded systems.

Setting Up a Real-Time Environment

Before writing a real-time application in Rust, it's essential to set up your development environment, focusing on tools that facilitate real-time system development.

1. Installing Rust

First, install Rust. The recommended way is to use `rustup`, which installs the Rust toolchain:

```bash
curl --proto '=https' --tlsv1.2 -sSf https://sh.rustup.rs | sh
```

2. Choosing Real-Time Libraries

Several libraries can aid in the development of real-time applications:

Tokio: An asynchronous runtime for Rust that provides the building blocks needed for writing scalable network applications.

RTIC: A framework for building real-time embedded systems in Rust, focusing on predictability and low overhead.

Actix: A powerful actor framework that can help manage stateful applications with real-time requirements.

3. Development Environment

Consider using an IDE with Rust support, such as Visual Studio Code with the Rust extension, which offers syntax highlighting, code completion, and debugging capabilities.

Key Concepts in Real-Time Programming with Rust
Tasks and Scheduling

In real-time systems, tasks can be categorized based on their priority. Implementing a scheduling mechanism is crucial to manage how tasks are executed:

Periodic Tasks: These tasks execute at regular intervals. Useful for systems requiring consistent behavior, like sensor polling.

Aperiodic Tasks: These tasks occur in response to specific events. They must be handled promptly but may not have a consistent execution pattern.

Using Rust, you can model these tasks using traits and structs to encapsulate behavior and properties such as priority and execution time.

Concurrency and Parallelism

Rust excels in safe concurrency. Real-time applications often involve multiple concurrent tasks that need to share resources without causing conflicts. You can achieve this through:

Mutexes: To secure access to shared resources.

Channels: For message-passing between tasks, allowing for safe data exchange without direct sharing.

By leveraging Rust's async/await syntax, you can create non-blocking I/O operations, making your real-time application responsive while handling multiple tasks concurrently.

Handling Time and Delays

In real-time systems, managing time accurately is essential. Use the `std::time` module to measure elapsed time, set timers, or schedule tasks. Carefully manage delays to ensure they conform to the application's real-time constraints.

Example: A Basic Real-Time Application

This example illustrates a simple real-time system that reads temperature data from a sensor and responds based on the readings.

Step 1: Defining Task Structures

```rust
struct TemperatureSensor{ temperature: f32,
```

```rust
}
impl TemperatureSensor {
fn read_temperature(&self) -> f32 {
// Simulate reading the temperature self.temperature
}
}
struct Alarm { threshold: f32,
}
impl Alarm {
fn trigger(&self) {
println!("Alarm triggered! Threshold exceeded: {}", self.threshold);
}
}
```

Step 2: Implementing the Main Loop

This main loop utilizes Rust's async features to read temperature data periodically.

```rust
use tokio::time::{sleep, Duration};
#[tokio::main] async fn main() {
let sensor = TemperatureSensor { temperature: 75.0 }; // Initial temperature let alarm = Alarm { threshold: 80.0 };
loop {
```

```rust
let    temperature    =    sensor.read_temperature();
println!("Current temperature: {}", temperature);

if temperature > alarm.threshold { alarm.trigger();
}

// Sleep for a while before the next reading
sleep(Duration::from_secs(1)).await;
}
}
```

Step 3: Running and Observing

Run the application with `cargo run`. Observe how it reads the temperature, checks against the threshold, and triggers an alarm when necessary. This simple model demonstrates how Rust can efficiently manage real- time tasks.

With its focus on safety, efficiency, and concurrency, Rust provides a robust framework for tackling the challenges of real-time programming. This chapter has laid the foundation for developing real-time applications, highlighting key concepts and providing practical examples.

Chapter 10: Using Rust to Develop IoT Applications at Scale

This chapter explores how Rust can be leveraged to develop IoT applications at scale, focusing on its features, ecosystem, and practical implementations.

10.1 The Promise of IoT and Its Challenges

IoT devices are becoming ubiquitous in various sectors such as healthcare, agriculture, smart cities, and industrial automation. These applications often require:

Low Latency: Real-time data processing and response.

Resource Efficiency: Limited memory and processing power on devices.

Security: Protection against vulnerabilities and unauthorized access.

Scalability: The ability to handle a growing number of devices and data streams.

However, developing reliable IoT solutions poses several challenges, such as handling concurrency, managing resource limitations, and ensuring memory safety. Rust's unique features position it well to tackle these issues.

10.2 Why Rust for IoT? ### 10.2.1 Performance

Rust offers performance comparable to C and C++, making it suitable for devices with constrained resources. Its zero-cost abstractions mean that developers can use high-level features without sacrificing speed.

10.2.2 Memory Safety

One of the foremost attributes of Rust is its ownership and borrowing system, which eliminates data races and socket leaks at compile time. This feature is invaluable in IoT applications where memory resources are limited, and stability is crucial.

10.2.3 Concurrency

Rust's concurrency model allows multiple tasks to be performed simultaneously without the risk of data corruption. This capability is essential for IoT applications where devices must handle multiple input streams and events concurrently.

10.2.4 Ecosystem Support

The Rust ecosystem is growing rapidly and includes libraries optimized for network communication, data serialization, and asynchronous programming. Notable libraries include:

Tokio: An asynchronous runtime for building networking applications.

Serde: A framework for serializing and deserializing Rust data structures.

Rust Embedded: A collection of tools and libraries aimed at embedded systems. ## 10.3 Developing Scalable IoT Applications with Rust

10.3.1 Setting Up Your Development Environment

Before diving into application development, set up the Rust development environment. This includes installing Rust through `rustup`, setting up your favorite IDE or code editor, and integrating necessary libraries.

10.3.2 Designing the Architecture

Effective IoT applications often employ a microservices architecture. Rust's strength in building small, efficient binaries aligns well with this approach. Here's how you might structure your architecture:

Edge Devices: Lightweight agents deployed on IoT devices to collect data.

Gateway: Serves as a bridge between edge devices and the cloud.

Cloud Services: Scalable backend services for data processing, storage, and analysis. ### 10.3.3 Example Use Case: Smart Farming

Consider a smart farming application where various sensors monitor soil moisture, temperature, and humidity. Using Rust, you might design the following components:

Sensor Firmware: Write efficient, low-level code to interact with sensors directly. Utilize libraries from the Rust Embedded ecosystem to handle GPIO, analog input, and communication protocols (e.g., I2C, SPI).

Data Collection and Reporting: Utilize the Tokio library for asynchronous communication with a central gateway, sending data at regular intervals without blocking.

Cloud Integration: Create RESTful APIs in Rust to receive data from gateways. Implement Serde to handle JSON serialization, making it easy to process incoming data streams.

Analytics and Alerting: Use Rust's type safety to process incoming data and trigger alerts based on predefined thresholds, ensuring farmers receive timely notifications.

10.3.4 Testing and Deployment

Testing is critical in IoT applications, as reliability can have real-world consequences. Use Rust's built-in testing framework to write unit and integration tests. For deployment, consider building Docker images for your services, leveraging Rust's compact binaries to optimize resource usage.

10.3.5 Ensuring Security

Security is paramount in IoT. Rust's ownership model aids in writing secure applications by eliminating common vulnerabilities related to memory usage. Implement additional security measures such as:

TLS: Use libraries like `rustls` to ensure secure communication between devices and services.

Firmware Updates: Implement secure OTA (over-the-air) update mechanisms to maintain device integrity.

10.4 Community and Resources

The Rust community is supportive and vibrant, continually expanding its library offerings and documentation. Engage with community resources such as:

The Rust Users Forum

The Rust Programming Language book

Online courses and workshops focused on Rust for embedded systems

By leveraging Rust's capabilities and ecosystem, developers can create robust solutions that not only meet today's IoT challenges but also pave the way for future innovations.

Modular Programming for Scalable IoT Solutions

With the surge in connected devices, it becomes imperative to design IoT solutions that are not only efficient and secure but also scalable. Rust, a systems programming language renowned for its performance and safety features, is an excellent candidate for developing scalable IoT solutions. This chapter delves into the principles of modular programming in Rust, exploring how these principles can be applied to create scalable IoT systems.

1. Understanding Modular Programming

Modular programming is an approach that emphasizes breaking down a program into smaller, manageable, and independently functioning pieces or modules. Each module encapsulates a specific piece of functionality, making the overall system easier to manage, extend, and maintain.

1.1 Benefits of Modular Programming

Here are some notable benefits of using modular programming in the context of IoT:

Encapsulation: Modules encapsulate their data and functionality, reducing dependencies and potential interactions between different parts of the system.

Reusability: Well-designed modules can be reused

across different projects, saving development time and resources.

Scalability: Modular systems are inherently easier to scale as new modules can be added or existing ones modified without significant changes to the entire system.

Improved Collaboration: Teams can work on different modules in parallel, increasing overall development speed and efficiency.

2. Rust and Its Unique Features

Rust is particularly suited for IoT development due to its focus on safety, concurrency, and performance. Some unique features of Rust include:

Memory Safety: Rust's ownership model prevents common memory-related vulnerabilities such as null pointer de-referencing and buffer overflows, crucial in the IoT realm, where devices often operate with limited resources.

Concurrency: Rust's concurrency model allows multiple threads to run without data races, facilitating the development of responsive IoT applications that need to handle many simultaneous connections or processes.

Rich Type System: Rust's type system enables developers to catch errors at compile-time rather than runtime, leading to more reliable and maintainable code.

3. Structuring an IoT Application in Rust

When developing an IoT application using Rust, it's essential to structure the application modularly. Below, we outline a high-level architecture showcasing how to break down an IoT application into modular components.

3.1 Defining Modules

A typical IoT application might consist of several modules, such as:

Device Management: Handles the registration, monitoring, and command processing of IoT devices.

Data Collection: Responsible for collecting sensor data and preparing it for transmission.

Communication: Manages network communication protocols (e.g., MQTT, CoAP) for device-to- device and device-to-cloud interaction.

Analytics: Processes and analyzes the collected data for insights and decision-making.

User Interface: Provides a visual or programmatic interface for users to interact with the system. ### 3.2 Sample Module Implementation

Here's a simple example of how one might define a module in Rust for data collection:

```rust
// src/data_collection.rs

pub struct Sensor { pub id: String, pub value: f64,
}

impl Sensor {

pub fn new(id: &str) -> Self {

Sensor { id: id.to_string(), value: 0.0 }

}

pub fn read(&mut self) -> f64 {
```

149

```
// Simulate reading a value (replace with actual sensor
reading logic) self.value = rand::random(); // Generate a
random value

self.value
}
}
```
` ` `

3.3 Integrating Modules

Once modules are defined, integrating them involves creating a cohesive system. This is typically done in the main application entry point:

```rust
// src/main.rs
mod data_collection;

use data_collection::Sensor; fn main() {
    let mut sensor = Sensor::new("TemperatureSensor1");


    loop {
        let value = sensor.read();
        println!("Sensor {} reads value: {}", sensor.id, value);
        // Here, you would add logic to transmit the value,
        process it, etc.
    }
}
```
` ` `

4. Managing Dependencies

In a modular system, managing dependencies effectively is critical. Rust's package manager, Cargo, allows developers to define dependencies in a `Cargo.toml` file, ensuring that each module can declare its requirements clearly. This promotes modularity and reduces the complexity of dependency management.

```toml [dependencies]

serde = "1.0"  # For data serialization

tokio = { version = "1.0", features = ["full"] }  # For asynchronous programming

```

5. Testing and Validation

Testing individual modules is vital for ensuring the reliability of the entire system. Rust's built-in testing framework allows developers to write unit tests for each module easily. Integrating Continuous Integration/Continuous Deployment (CI/CD) pipelines ensures that all modules are tested collectively before deployment.

5.1 Writing Tests

Here's an example of how to write a test for the `Sensor` module:

```rust
// src/data_collection.rs
#[cfg(test)] mod tests {
use super::*;
```

```
#[test]
fn test_sensor_read() {
let mut sensor = Sensor::new("TestSensor"); let value =
sensor.read();
assert!(value >= 0.0 && value <= 1.0);  // Assuming read
should return a value between 0.0 and 1.0
}
}
```

By leveraging Rust's unique features such as memory safety, concurrency, and a rich type system, developers can create robust, efficient, and maintainable systems. This chapter provided an overview of the principles of modular programming, how to structure a Rust-based IoT application, and emphasized the importance of testing and managing dependencies. As the IoT landscape continues to evolve, adopting modular programming practices in Rust will undoubtedly facilitate the development of scalable and resilient IoT solutions.

Best Practices for Debugging and Testing in Rust

In this chapter, we will explore various best practices for debugging and testing in Rust programming, helping developers utilize Rust's powerful features to create robust applications.

1. Understanding Rust's Compiler and Error Messages

Rust's compiler is renowned for its informative and descriptive error messages. When a program does not compile, the compiler usually provides detailed explanations of what went wrong and suggestions for fixing it.

Best Practice:

Read Error Messages Carefully: Spend time analyzing compiler errors. Often, they contain hints about the nature of the bug and where it occurs. Rust's compiler is designed to help developers by pointing to the exact line of code and providing context for the issue.

2. Leveraging the Rust Standard Library

Rust's standard library provides a wealth of utilities and structures that can help streamline debugging. ### Best Practice:

Utilize `Debug` Traits: Every type in Rust can implement the `Debug` trait, which allows for convenient formatting of instances using the `{:?}` formatter. Use this to print the state of your variables while debugging, making your output clear and informative.

```rust
#[derive(Debug)] struct MyStruct {

value: i32,

}

fn main() {

let data = MyStruct { value: 42 }; println!("{:?}", data);

}
```

3. Using Logging

While debugging is primarily about finding bugs, logging is about understanding application behavior. The

`log` crate can provide a flexible framework for logging in Rust applications.

Best Practice:

Incorporate Logging: Use the `log` crate to emit logs at various levels (e.g., info, debug, error). This can help track down issues in production and provide context about application performance and behavior.

```rust
use log::{info, warn};

fn example_function() {
    info!("This is an informational message");


    warn!("This is a warning message");
}
```

4. Unit Testing and Integration Testing

Rust's built-in testing framework simplifies the process of writing both unit tests and integration tests. ### Best Practice:

Write Comprehensive Tests: Always write unit tests for individual functions and integration tests for modules. Aim for a high test coverage percentage but keep in mind that meaningful tests should focus on edge cases and expected behavior.

```rust
#[cfg(test)] mod tests {
#[test]
fn test_addition() { assert_eq!(2 + 2, 4);
}
}
```

5. Continuous Testing with `cargo test`

Rust's package manager, Cargo, includes built-in support for running tests. ### Best Practice:

Use Cargo for Testing: Regularly run your tests using `cargo test`. Integrate this step into your development workflow and consider setting up continuous integration (CI) pipelines to ensure tests run on code submissions.

6. Debugging with IDEs

Modern Integrated Development Environments (IDEs) like Visual Studio Code, IntelliJ Rust, or Eclipse with Rust plugins provide powerful debugging tools.

Best Practice:

Use IDE Debuggers: Take advantage of IDE features such as breakpoints, step-through debugging, and variable watches to diagnose issues more effectively than just using print statements.

7. Profiling Tools

Performance issues can often be harder to identify than logic errors. Rust offers profiling tools to help diagnose these concerns.

Best Practice:

Profile Your Code: Use tools available in Rust's ecosystem (e.g., `cargo flamegraph`, `cargo profiler`) to analyze performance and identify bottlenecks in your application.

8. Handling Panics Gracefully

Panics can lead to unexpected application crashes. Rust provides tools to handle these gracefully.

Best Practice:

Use `Result` and `Option` Types: Instead of allowing panics, handle errors explicitly using `Result` and `Option` types to enforce proper error handling and prevent unexpected crashes.

```rust
fn safe_divide(a: f64, b: f64) -> Result<f64, String> { if b == 0.0 {

Err(String::from("Division by zero"))

} else {

Ok(a / b)

}

}
```

9. Use External Crates Wisely

Rust has a vibrant ecosystem of external crates that can enhance debugging and testing capabilities. ### Best Practice:

Utilize Crates for Enhanced Functionality: Consider using crates like `assert_eq`, `mockito` for testing HTTP requests, or `serenity` for logging, depending on your application's needs.

By adopting best practices such as leveraging the compiler's error messages, utilizing logging, writing comprehensive tests, and using sophisticated IDE features, developers can create high-quality, maintainable Rust applications. Rust's strict compile-time checks, combined with powerful built-in and external tools, equip developers with everything they need to address and resolve issues effectively.

Conclusion

As we conclude our journey through "Rust Programming for IoT: The Complete Guide to Developing Secure and Efficient Smart Devices," it's clear that the intersection of Rust and the Internet of Things is not just a technological trend, but a significant step forward in creating robust, secure, and efficient smart devices. Through this guide, we've explored the fundamental principles of Rust programming, its powerful features, and how they can be effectively harnessed to develop IoT applications that stand the test of time and security challenges.

Throughout the chapters, we've delved into the unique characteristics of Rust, such as its memory safety, concurrency, and performance. We've seen how these features address common vulnerabilities encountered in the IoT landscape, thus reducing the risks associated with deploying smart devices in real-world environments. By adopting Rust, developers can write code that not only performs well but also minimizes the chances of critical failures due to security oversights.

Moreover, the practical examples and projects included in this guide have demonstrated how to apply Rust in various IoT contexts—whether you're building sensors, gateways, or even full-fledged smart systems. The hands-on approach encourages you to explore, experiment, and gain confidence in your Rust programming skills, empowering you to bring your IoT ideas to life.

As we move forward in an increasingly connected world, the demand for secure and efficient devices will only grow. It is our hope that this guide equips you with the knowledge and tools necessary to excel in this rapidly evolving field. Rust is more than just a programming language; it represents a paradigm shift towards developing sustainable and reliable IoT solutions.

In closing, we encourage you to continue your exploration of Rust and IoT. Engage with the community, contribute to open-source projects, and stay abreast of the latest developments in both realms. By doing so, you will not only enhance your skills but also play a crucial role in shaping the future of smart devices.

Thank you for joining us on this journey, and we wish you success in all your Rust programming endeavors in the IoT space!

Biography

Jeff Stuart is a visionary writer and seasoned web developer with a passion for crafting dynamic and user-centric web applications. With years of hands-on experience in the tech industry, Jeff has mastered the art of problem-solving through code, specializing in Rust programming and cutting-edge web technologies. His expertise lies in creating efficient, scalable, and secure solutions that push the boundaries of what web applications can achieve.

As a lifelong learner and tech enthusiast, Jeff thrives on exploring the ever-evolving landscape of programming languages and frameworks. When he's not immersed in writing code or brainstorming innovative ideas, you'll find him sharing his knowledge through inspiring content that empowers others to unlock their full potential in the digital world.

Beyond his professional pursuits, Jeff enjoys exploring the art of minimalist design, reading thought-provoking books on technology and philosophy, and hiking to recharge his creative energies. His unwavering dedication to excellence and his belief in the transformative power of technology shine through in every page of his work, making this book a compelling guide for anyone eager to master the art of Rust programming and web development.

Glossary: Rust Programming for IoT

A

Async/Await: A programming pattern allowing functions to be paused and resumed, facilitating the handling of asynchronous operations. In IoT, this can be crucial for managing operations that involve waiting for network responses or sensor data.

B

Bare Metal: Programming that runs directly on hardware without an operating system. Rust's performance characteristics make it an excellent choice for bare-metal programming in IoT devices.

C

Cargo: Rust's package manager and build system. Cargo helps manage dependencies, run builds, and distribute libraries, which is particularly useful for IoT projects that can involve numerous libraries and dependencies.

Concurrency: The ability of an application to manage multiple tasks simultaneously. Rust's ownership model ensures safe concurrency without data races, making it suitable for IoT systems with multiple interacting components.

D

Device Firmware: Software programmed onto a hardware device that controls its functions. In IoT, writing efficient firmware using Rust can enhance system reliability and performance.

E

Embedded Systems: Computers designed to perform dedicated functions within larger systems. Rust is increasingly popular for developing embedded systems in IoT due to its safety and performance characteristics.

F

First-Class Functions: Functions that can be passed as arguments, returned from other functions, and assigned to variables. This concept is crucial in Rust for developing modular and reusable code, important in IoT applications.

G

GLibc: The GNU C Library, often used as a standard C library for Linux-based systems. Rust can be employed alongside GLibc in IoT applications where a Linux environment is present.

H

Hardware Abstraction Layer (HAL): A layer of code that abstracts low-level hardware operations, allowing higher-level software to interact with hardware components without needing to know the specifics of the hardware. Rust provides several libraries to facilitate HAL development in IoT projects.

I

IoT Gateway: A device that acts as a bridge between IoT devices and the cloud or internet. Rust can be used to develop lightweight and efficient IoT gateways that process and relay data to the cloud.

L

Lifetime: A concept in Rust that refers to how long references are valid in the program. Understanding lifetimes is essential for memory safety, especially in IoT applications that manage multiple sensors and devices.

M

Microcontroller: A compact integrated circuit designed to govern a specific operation in an embedded system. Rust can be used to write efficient code for microcontrollers, making it an attractive option for IoT developers.

Middleware: Software that connects different applications or services. In IoT, middleware can enhance communication and data management, and Rust's performance allows for efficient middleware solutions.

N

No-std: A mode in Rust that allows programming without access to the Rust standard library, necessary for embedded systems with limited resources. `no-std` is widely used in IoT development where memory and processing power are constrained.

P

Protocols: Established sets of rules for communication between devices. Rust supports various protocols relevant to IoT, including MQTT and CoAP, allowing for effective data exchange.

Panic: In Rust, a panic occurs when a program encounters an unrecoverable error. Understanding how Rust handles panics is vital, especially in IoT applications where continuous operation is critical.

R

Rustacean: A term affectionately used to refer to Rust programmers. It symbolizes the community around the Rust programming language, which is particularly important for developers collaborating on IoT projects.

S

Safety: Rust's core principle emphasizes memory safety, which refers to preventing bugs and vulnerabilities that could compromise system integrity. This is particularly important in IoT, where devices often operate in critical environments.

Sensor Fusion: The process of combining multiple sensor readings to produce more accurate and reliable information. Rust's performance can enhance algorithms used in sensor fusion for IoT applications.

T

Thread Safety: A guarantee that data structures are safe to use in multi-threaded contexts without risking data corruption. Rust's design ensures thread safety, which is beneficial for concurrent IoT operations.

U

User Space: The memory area where user processes execute, as opposed to kernel space. In IoT applications running on Linux-based systems, understanding user space vs. kernel space is significant for resource management.

W

WebAssembly (Wasm): A binary instruction format for a stack-based virtual machine, enabling high-performance applications on web pages. Rust can compile to WebAssembly, making it useful for developing IoT applications that require web interaction.

www.ingramcontent.com/pod-product-compliance
Lightning Source LLC
LaVergne TN
LVHW051340050326
832903LV00031B/3652